BUDDHISTS IN

Denise Cush

Hodder & Stoughton

LONDON SYDNEY AUCKLAND TORONTO

British Library Cataloguing in Publication Data
Cush, Denise
  Buddhists in Britain today.
  1. Great Britain. Buddhism
  I. Title II. Series
  294.30941

  ISBN 0 340 51948 7

First published 1990

Typeset by Wearside Tradespools, Fulwell, Sunderland
Printed in Great Britain for the educational publishing division of
Hodder and Stoughton Ltd, Mill Road, Dunton Green, Sevenoaks,
Kent by Page Bros (Norwich) Ltd

Contents

—

Section 3: Further study 117

Preface

—

This book attempts to give an authentic picture of Buddhism in the United Kingdom. Most of the interviews have been checked by the interviewees. Some have been checked for doctrinal accuracy by leading authorities in the tradition; thanks are due to Ven. Dhammavijitha of the London Buddhist Vihara for looking at the Goonewardene family interview. Other interviewees are themselves leading teachers within their traditions. The remainder are offered as purely personal viewpoints. Any remaining errors are my own responsibility.

I would like to thank all who consented to be interviewed and spared time to answer all my questions. I am also grateful to the Buddhist Society of Great Britain for its helpful publication, the *Buddhist Directory*, which enabled me to make many of the contacts. Many thanks are due to the members of the Buddhism Resource Project who made constructive suggestions and provided support and encouragement. Thanks also to Carol Miles for helping out with the word-processing when time was short, and finally to David and my family for their practical support.

Denise Cush

section one

INTRODUCTION

—

About this book

—

All words contained in the Glossary on pp. 133–137 are shown in italics on their first appearance in the text.

There are many books in which you can read about the life of the *Buddha*, the main teachings of Buddhism and the history of the development of Buddhism in India and in the Far Eastern countries to which Buddhism spread. Some of these are listed in the Bibliography on pp. 124–130. However, sometimes if we just read about it in books Buddhism can seem long ago, far away and of interest only to monks and scholars. In fact Buddhism is a living force affecting the daily lives of many people in our country today.

The number of Buddhists in Britain is growing every year and so it is likely that you will meet Buddhists. Perhaps you are a Buddhist yourself. If you do not know any Buddhists and would like to arrange to meet a Buddhist, or perhaps have a Buddhist speaker talk to your group, there is a list of addresses to contact on pp. 131–132.

This book is based on interviews undertaken between 1987 and 1989 with ten practising Buddhists living in Britain. As with most other religions there are several different traditions within Buddhism, and the interviews were chosen to give a selection from the rich variety which is Buddhism in Britain today. You will find that Buddhists do not always believe exactly the same things or follow the same customs; this may be confusing but it makes life more interesting! Each person is an individual rather than a 'typical Buddhist' and all are working out for themselves their own way of life as the Buddha recommended.

Before you read on, you might find it a useful exercise to jot down what you already know about Buddhism, what images spring to mind when you hear the words 'Buddha' and 'Buddhism'. What image do you have of a 'typical Buddhist'? You might like to share these ideas and/or record them in writing. Then you can see if your ideas have changed when you have finished reading this book.

About Buddhism

—

■ BUDDHIST COUNTRIES ■

Buddhism is one of the major religious traditions of the human race, a worldwide religion with hundreds of millions of followers in the world today. It has a history of 2,500 years and has had a profound influence on the culture of India and the countries of the Far East. The *Dharma*, as many Buddhists call their religion, was first proclaimed in India where it was influential until about the twelfth century *CE*. Countries where Buddhism has been traditional include Sri Lanka, Burma, Thailand, Cambodia, Laos, China, Japan, Korea, Mongolia, Tibet, Nepal, Sikkim, Bhutan and Vietnam. Several of these countries, such as Burma, Thailand and Sri Lanka, continue to have a large majority of their population loyal to Buddhism. In Japan, Buddhism flourishes alongside other religions, and even in the countries which have become communist there is evidence that the religion is still important to people, for example in Laos and Tibet. In recent times Buddhism has spread to the USA, Europe and Australasia and has genuinely become a 'world religion'.

> Look up these countries in an atlas. What do you know about any of these countries?

■ THE BUDDHA ■

Although to a Buddhist the Dharma is an eternal truth, Buddhism in its historical form began with the teaching of an Indian prince called *Siddhartha Gautama* who lived in the sixth or fifth century *BCE*. Although he was brought up in luxury, this did not bring him lasting happiness as he wondered about the meaning of life, especially the reason for and answer to pain, decay and death. He left home and spent six years trying to find the answer by listening to religious teachers and practising traditional techniques such as *meditation* and *asceticism* (e.g. fasting). Finally, through deep meditation, he gained

4

insight into the truth about life, the cause of suffering and death, and the way in which to deal with suffering and death. This is known as his 'enlightenment', and so he is referred to as 'the Enlightened One' or 'the Buddha'. He spent the rest of his life teaching others how to reach truth, peace and happiness, and he founded communities of monks, nuns and laypeople to continue his work.

Find out more about the Buddha's life from the books and videos listed in the Bibliography on pp. 124–130.

■ THE BASIC TEACHINGS OF BUDDHISM ■

Buddhism is unique among the major world religions because it is based not upon belief in God but upon human experience and human potential. It is usually counted as a religion because it believes that human life has a meaning and purpose which goes beyond the material world that we can perceive with our senses. It puts forward certain truths about life and ways of behaving. Buddhism has never had a set list of beliefs which it asks people to accept with blind faith, because it stresses that individuals must discover the truth in their own experience. If you follow the way of life recommended by the Buddha, you will gradually see into the truth about life and can also eventually become enlightened. However, there are certain basic beliefs that Buddhists share which are based on the teachings of the Buddha and to varying extents on their own experience.

- Life as most of us live it is unsatisfactory, because it contains suffering and because nothing lasts.
- Much suffering is caused by the ignorance and selfishness of people, who are filled with greed and craving for things which do not last and do not bring lasting happiness.
- Like everything else, we ourselves are continually changing, both from life to life and day to day. There is no 'inner self', 'soul' or 'real me' that stays the same.
- The changes and suffering in our lives can be blamed on no one else, but are the results of our own thoughts and actions. As long as our thoughts and actions come from a mind which is ignorant and selfish, we will be unhappy.
- If through following the way of life recommended by the Buddha, through discovering the truth, acting morally and practising meditation, we can purify our mind and rid ourselves of greed,

hatred and delusion, then an alternative state of being called 'enlightenment' or *nirvana* can be achieved. This is what the Buddha achieved in his lifetime. It is hard to imagine, but involves perfect happiness and peace, understanding of life, unselfish love and no longer having to be reborn into lives of suffering. In *Mahayana* Buddhism this is referred to as 'becoming Buddha'.

• Most Buddhists believe that this whole process goes beyond our present life and that while we remain selfish and ignorant we are continually reborn into this state of life every time we die. On the other hand, if we achieve nirvana, at death we will enter a timeless state of peace. Other Buddhists, however, consider the belief in rebirth to be less essential and prefer to concentrate on this life.

Buddha's teaching was at first passed down orally, and many of his teachings were put into lists to aid memory. Here are some of the most important lists.

THE FOUR NOBLE TRUTHS

1 All life involves suffering and is unsatisfactory.
2 The origin of suffering is selfish desire and clinging to things that do not last.
3 If selfish desire and clinging can be stopped, suffering will stop, leaving nirvana.
4 The way to stop suffering is to follow the *Eightfold Path*.

THE EIGHTFOLD PATH

1 Right view
2 Right intention
3 Right speech
4 Right conduct
5 Right livelihood
6 Right effort
7 Right mindfulness
8 Right contemplation

THE THREE MARKS OF LIFE

1 *Dukkha*: All life involves suffering.
2 *Anicca*: All life is impermanent.
3 *Anatta*: There is no unchanging 'soul' or 'self'.

THE FIVE MORAL PRECEPTS

I undertake to abstain from the following:

1 Killing
2 Taking what is not given
3 Sensual misconduct
4 False speech
5 Intoxicants that cloud the mind

- Discover and learn the meaning of the following central Buddhist concepts: dukkha, anicca, anatta, *samsara*, nirvana, *karma* and Buddha. Brief definitions of these terms are given in the Glossary at the back of this book (pp. 133–137) and more detailed explanations can be found in the books listed in the Bibliography (pp. 124–130, especially, 3, 11, 34, 35, 36).

■ THE VARIETIES OF BUDDHISM ■

There are many varieties of Buddhism because it has never been a dogmatic religion; it allows people to see the truths about life for themselves rather than forcing them to accept a list of beliefs without question. It has also been very flexible and adaptable throughout its history, developing different customs to suit different people in different places.

People tend to divide present-day Buddhism into two main forms: *Theravada* and *Mahayana*. Theravada, or 'the way of the elders', is followed in the more southern countries, Sri Lanka, Burma, Thailand, Laos and Cambodia. Mahayana, or 'the great vehicle', is an overall term for the variety of traditons followed in the more northern countries, China, Japan, Korea, Vietnam, Tibet, Mongolia, Sikkim and Bhutan. There is also a third form *Vajrayana*, which is important in Tibetan Buddhism.

THERAVADA BUDDHISM

Theravada is the only surviving tradition of about eighteen early non-Mahayana schools of Buddhism. As the name suggests, Theravada prides itself on a long unbroken tradition of teaching. The Theravada Buddhists have a collection of scriptures known as the *Pali Canon*, written down in about the first century BCE, which preserves the oral tradition of the teaching of the Buddha. Theravada Buddhism stresses the Buddha as a human teacher. He is precious because buddhas who discover the truth about life are very rare; most people are incapable of discovering this truth for themselves and are reliant on the teachings of the Buddha. Nevertheless, each person is responsible for his or her own salvation and has to follow the teachings for him/herself. As a preserver of the tradition, of teachers and of examples, the monastic *Sangha* or community is also precious. Hence Buddhists 'take refuge' in 'three precious things': the Buddha, the Dharma and the Sangha. Theravada lays great emphasis on meditation.

MAHAYANA BUDDHISM

Mahayana Buddhists consider that they belong to a more all-embracing form of Buddhism than that which was taught by the early non-Mahayana schools; they sometimes refer to the latter as *Hinayana* or 'small vehicle' Buddhism. Some scholars see Mahayana as a development of Buddhism which occurred several hundred years after the Buddha lived, as perhaps a spiritual revival, but Mahayana Buddhists themselves consider their teachings to be the true message of the Buddha rather than any later development. These teachings are contained in a large variety of Mahayana *sutras* or scriptures. These scriptures contain ideas rather different from those of the Theravada Pali Canon. It is stressed that everyone has the potential to become a buddha, an enlightened being. Buddhists are encouraged to strive to become buddhas not for their own sake, but because buddhas can help to save others. Anyone seriously following this resolve is called a *bodhisattva* or 'being of enlighten-ment'. An important result of this is that people can pray for help to beings who are further advanced on this path than themselves. This includes both advanced human teachers, or *gurus*, and bodhisattvas visualised as heavenly beings. Mahayana Buddhists also have a somewhat different way of looking at the Buddha. The human Buddha who lived and died was only one form of the eternal Buddha who has no beginning or end.

There have been many different forms of Mahayana Buddhism as Buddhism has developed in India, Tibet, China and Japan. Influential traditions in Britain have been *Zen* Buddhism, Tibetan Buddhism, *Nichiren* Buddhism, the Western Buddhist Order (*WBO*) and to a lesser extent *Pure Land* Buddhism.

Zen Buddhism

Zen Buddhism developed in China, Korea and Japan. It emphasises a direct transmission of the teaching from the teacher to the pupil rather than in the written word. Meditation is stressed as the central practice on the way to enlightenment. The word 'zen' is in fact simply Japanese for meditation. Zen Buddhism, with its love of simplicity and nature, has had a great influence on Japanese and Chinese art and culture, including *calligraphy*, painting, poetry and the martial arts. There are two main surviving traditions within Zen: *Rinzai*, famous for the *koans* or deep, riddle-like sayings of its masters, and *Soto* which stresses quiet meditation or serene reflection.

Tibetan Buddhism

Tibetan Buddhism developed its own beliefs and customs, partly as a result of the geographical location of Tibet. It is basically Mahayana Buddhism with the addition of elements of *Tantric* Buddhism or Vajrayana, a form of Buddhism which developed its own scriptures and practices in India from the fourth century CE onwards. Among the characteristics of this form of Buddhism are *mantras* or powerful phrases or syllables, *mandalas* or circular coloured diagrams, *mudras* or symbolic shapes made with the hands, and a large variety of rituals and meditation practices. Tibetan Buddhists place great importance on bodhisattvas and upon human gurus or *lamas* who pass on the precious teachings. Some of the more important lamas are believed to be reincarnations of holy teachers who lived in earlier ages and to be bodhisattvas living on earth to help others. The scriptures of Tibetan Buddhism are vast, including both Hinayana and Mahayana sutras, *tantras* and other writings. There are four main surviving traditions of Tibetan Buddhism, known as the *Nying ma pa*, the *Sakya pa*, and *Kargyu pa* and the *Ge lug pa*. These have different lines of lamas and different customs. Tibetan Buddhism provides a variety of rituals and forms of meditation.

Pure Land Buddhism

Pure Land Buddhism developed in China and Japan. It is a simple form of Buddhism based on one particular Mahayana sutra which describes the Pure Land of the heavenly Buddha Amitabha or *Amida*. Amida is not the historical Buddha who lived and died on this earth but another enlightened one who dwells in a paradise land and will help all those who pray to him. Faith in Amida Buddha leads to being reborn in this paradise land where it will be easy to practise Buddhism and gain enlightenment. Pure Land Buddhism has not gained a very large following in Britain.

Nichiren Buddhism

Nichiren was a thirteenth-century Buddhist teacher who felt that Buddhism had become corrupt in his day. He called people back to what he saw as true Buddhism, the teaching contained in the Mahayana sutra known as the Lotus of the Wonderful Law. This scripture stresses the eternity of Buddha *Shakyamuni* and his tender love for all beings, together with the teaching that all beings have the potential to become buddhas. The central practice of Nichiren Buddhism is the reciting of the mantra 'namo myoho rengye kyo'. These Japanese words literally mean 'homage to the lotus of the wonderful law' but this literal translation can miss the point that the actual chanting puts one in touch with the law of the universe, that of cause and effect. There are several traditions of Nichiren, the most influential in Britain being *Nichiren Shoshu*, known in Japan as the *lay* organisation *Soka Gakkai*. Nichiren Shoshu stresses that reciting the mantra, together with the practice of a Buddhist way of life, has practical results as well as long-term spiritual ones.

WBO

The WBO (Western Buddhist Order and the *FWBO* (Friends of the Western Buddhist Order) were founded as recently as 1967 by an Englishman, the Venerable Sangharakshita. Although basically Mahayana in outlook, the movement stresses the basic unity of all forms of Buddhism and the spirit of Buddhism rather than the collections of oriental customs that have grown up around it. The Western Buddhist Order itself is a new way of taking Buddhist practice seriously providing ordination which does not necessarily involve adopting the lifestyle of a monk or nun. It sees itself as a practical form of Buddhism suited to the modern world, especially to those brought up in a 'Western' culture.

■ BUDDHISM IN BRITAIN ■

Although Buddhism is 2,500 years old, it is a very new religion in the United Kingdom. In earlier centuries a few travellers and missionaries reached Buddhist countries, but no serious study was made of Buddhist teachings until the late nineteenth century during the expansion of the British Empire into countries like Sri Lanka where Buddhism was practised. In 1879 Edwin Arnold, who had been teaching in India, published a poem based on the Buddha's life called 'The Light of Asia', which helped spread the Buddha's name among English-speaking people. T.W. Rhys Davids, who had been in the Ceylon (Sri Lankan) civil service, formed the *Pali* text society in 1881 which for the first time collected, published and translated the Theravada Buddhist scriptures. At this time the interest in Buddhism was an academic and scholarly one. None of these early scholars of Buddhism seriously considered becoming practising Buddhists, although they admired the rational philosophy and moral teachings of Buddhism. The scholars' emphasis on the philosophical and intellectual side of Buddhism has led some people to think that Buddhism is too difficult to understand!

The first interest in Buddhism as a possible way of life occurred at the beginning of the twentieth century. The first British man to be ordained a Buddhist monk was Alan Bennett, in Burma in 1898. He returned to Britain in 1907 and a small Buddhist society began. These first Buddhists were supported by the *Theosophical Society*, including the influential Christmas Humphreys. A few Sri Lankan monks came to settle in Britain. In 1926 Christmas Humphreys and others formed the Buddhist Lodge, which became the Buddhist Society of Great Britain in 1943. This society catered both for people who wanted to practise Buddhism and for those who were 'just interested'. These early British Buddhists have been criticised for seeing Buddhism as a set of interesting ideas to discuss rather than as a new way to live your life, and for interpreting Buddhism to suit themselves, but at least they made it possible for British people to find out about Buddhism. In the period up to 1939, British Buddhists had most contact with Theravada Buddhism, mainly because the countries of the British Empire, such as Sri Lanka and Burma, were Theravada and because the first scriptures to be translated were the Pali Canon. British people today therefore tend to know more about Theravada and to see it as somehow the 'true' or most basic Buddhism. There are rather more Theravada Buddhist centres in Britain in the 1980s than of any other tradition.

The first book in English on Japanese Zen Buddhism was published by D.T. Suzuki in 1927. The interest in Japanese Buddhism increased during and after the Second World War. Christmas Humphreys published popular paperbacks on Zen in 1947 and 1951. Interest in Zen was also stimulated when it became fashionable among some young people in the USA in the 1950s – the so-called 'beatniks' or 'beat generation'. Zen ideas influenced the American writer Jack Kerouac among others. More serious Buddhists criticised this interest as a superficial fashion which involved no real understanding of Buddhism, but it did mean that Buddhism reached a wider public. Pure Land Buddhism also came to Britain from Japan in the 1950s, but it has not proved to be as popular as Zen Buddhism.

The 1960s and 1970s brought Tibetan Buddhism and the WBO to British notice. In 1959 the *Dalai Lama* and leading teachers fled Tibet which had been invaded by China in 1951. Tibetan teachings were then spread in Britain, the rest of Europe, Australasia and the

USA. The colourful art and rituals of Tibetan Buddhism appealed to young people at a time when Indian and Eastern culture was fashionable among the so-called hippies. As with the beatniks before them, some of this interest in Buddhism was not very serious and was rather shocking to traditional Buddhists. For example, meditation experiences were compared by Timothy Leary to the experiences induced by psychedelic drugs. However, some people who took an interest in Buddhism just because it was fashionable later took it seriously. Some of today's committed Buddhists first met Buddhism while on the 'hippy trail' through India and Nepal.

In 1967 Sangharakshita founded the WBO in Britain, the first Buddhist tradition to begin in the country. Although still very new, the WBO has established itself as a valid tradition of Buddhism which is well suited to British culture and forms a significant part of the presence of Buddhism in the country today.

The 1970s and 1980s have seen the introduction and growing popularity of Nichiren Buddhism in Britain. The emphasis on practical results in terms of material as well as spiritual success seems to suit current expectations which are perhaps more 'materialistic' or 'realistic' than the ideals of the 1960s. Several celebrities from the television and pop worlds follow Nichiren Buddhism. As with Zen in the 1950s and Tibetan Buddhism in the 1960s and 1970s, Nichiren Buddhism seems to be going through a period of being in fashion.

At the time of writing, Buddhism, a religion that was virtually unheard of in Britain a hundred years ago, seems now to be well established. All the main traditions of Buddhism have followers and have become well organised. Unlike the majority of Muslims, Hindus or Sikhs in Britain, the majority of British Buddhists are ethnically British, and are usually converts rather than from Buddhist families. There has been no large-scale immigration from Buddhist countries, although some families from Buddhist countries have settled in Britain.

Buddhism is steadily growing in the number of its followers. In 1981 the Buddhist Society could give addresses for 76 Buddhist centres, in 1983 for 107, and in 1988 for 188. It is also consolidating itself. Many of the traditions which started by attracting fashionable interest now have an established, serious membership of a variety of ages, and sufficient funds to run large centres and courses. We are beginning to see a second generation of children who are born to Buddhist parents and a need to consider their educational requirements. Buddhism is now part of the syllabus in many universities, colleges and schools. There are A level and GCSE examination papers in Buddhism, and teachers are looking at aspects of Buddhism with primary-age children. However, Buddhism in Britain is still very new and as yet a minority interest. Its influence, however, is wider than just those people who would call themselves Buddhists, and includes a sizeable number of people who are just interested or find some of the ideas of Buddhism attractive.

section two

THE

INTERVIEWS

—

The following reports of how individual Buddhists practise their tradition are based on interviews conducted by the author between 1987 and 1989.

1

VAJIRA BAILEY:
the science of Buddhism (Soto Zen)

Vajira Bailey lives in Birmingham. In her pleasant house overlooking a park she has made one of the rooms into a *zendo* or shrine room. Vajira leads a group of Soto Zen Buddhists who meet regularly at her home.

Vajira has always worked in scientific areas and finds the Buddhist approach to life a practical, scientific one:

> You don't have to accept dogma or beliefs, but try the method and see if it works. In my case meditation had an immediate positive effect on me.

Buddhist teachings, like science, help to make sense of the things that happen in life:

> Once, when I was 18, walking home late in the evening, I had a wonderful experience as if I could see the unity of all things in the universe and their interdependence, a deep experience which changed my views and stayed with me. The phrase that seemed to sum up the experience is 'there are no edges'. This is very personal and hard to describe, but when I later studied Buddhism at evening classes, I realised that it was what Zen teachers call *satori* – those special moments when you glimpse into the heart of existence.

The type of meditation practised in Soto Zen is called *zazen* or 'sitting meditation':

> The idea is to practise serene reflection; this means simply sitting observing what arises, that is your thoughts, without getting caught up in them like we usually do. It's rather like watching buses go by but not getting on them.

There is also *kinhin* or walking meditation, in which one concentrates the mind upon walking in a slow, calm, aware manner. Regular practice of zazen or kinhin helps you to become a calmer person with more insight into life and awareness of how to live it:

> Meditation has given me greater clarity of mind, and gradually changed my attitudes and way of life. It is easy to have faith and confidence in Buddhist practice because you can actually see it working.

Vajira has been a Buddhist for a long time, since 1964. Like many British Buddhists, she tried different traditions until she found the one that felt right for her:

> When you find your teacher, you know that this is right for you.

In Zen Buddhism it is considered vital to have a personal teacher; the experience of the truth about life must be passed directly from teacher to pupil as it is impossible to put into written words. Vajira's teacher is Roshi (Reverend Master) Jiyu Kennett, who made history by becoming a female Zen master, the first Western woman to do it. In Soto Zen, men and women can become monks. In Japan they are called *unsui* which means 'free as the clouds'. Vajira herself has taken lay ordination or *jukai*, which means a serious commitment to Buddhist practice. The ceremony involves receiving a *ketchimyaku* or scroll on which are written all the names of the ancestors or lineage of teachers in an unbroken line from Buddha Shakyamuni to your own teacher. Your own name is added to the list and a line drawn straight back to the Buddha.

Another aspect of jukai is receiving the Ten Precepts of the Zen Buddhist way of life. These are:

1 Do not kill.
2 Do not steal.
3 Do not covet.
4 Do not say that which is not true.
5 Do not sell the wine of delusion.
6 Do not speak against others.
7 Do not be proud of yourself and devalue others.
8 Do not be mean in giving the Dharma or wealth.
9 Do not be angry.
10 Do not defame the Three Jewels (the Buddha, the Dharma and the Sangha).

Following these precepts affects everything you do. In Vajira's case, it affects her choice of career:

> I have always worked in scientific fields including atomic energy research, paint research and soil mechanics. Because Buddhism is based on non-harming I could no longer be involved with atomic energy research because of the possibility of making destructive weapons that this knowledge gives rise to, and because of the real dangers to the environment.

Instead she prefers to work in areas of science that directly help people, such as in a foetal monitoring clinic, in a pathology laboratory screening cervical smears and in acupunture:

> I am not an active campaigner against nuclear weapons. The only way to change the world is to change our inner selves and then the outside world will look after itself. However I can find no justification for nuclear weapons or indeed weapons of any kind.

As you practise Buddhism, your daily life also changes:

> Although I'm not totally vegetarian, I find that I eat less and less meat and do not like cooking it at all. I know that everything has Buddha nature within it, even stones and atoms. This leads to respect for all things.

There is less need for escapism and distraction:

> I find that I rarely drink alcohol and hardly ever go to the cinema.

In other words, moral precepts are not a matter of will power. Rather, by practising zazen, unskilful, unnecessary or harmful action diminishes naturally. You know what is wrong by the uncomfortable feeling you get. This leads you to avoid such action.

Vajira leads a group of Soto Zen Buddhists who meet weekly in the zendo in her house. She usually wears black because it feels right (it is the colour of rest) and a black *wakesa* or little stole around her neck. This is like a diminutive monk's robe and is a symbol of her training and ordination. The zendo contains a shrine with statues of the Buddha, the embodiment of enlightened mind, and the bodhisattva Kanzeon, the embodiment of compassion. There are also candles, artificial silk flowers, incense, bells, clappers and an *ihai* or memoral tablet for a dead friend and his wife (a Japanese custom). There are also *zafus* (cushions) for meditation, a picture of Roshi Kennett and a large temple bowl gong which belongs to one of the group. Meetings consist of zazen and kinhin, reading the teachings of Zen masters such as *Dogen*, who founded Soto Zen in the eleventh century CE, reciting favourite Mahayana sutras, listening to taped talks from modern Zen teachers, discussion and tea.

There are special festivals and customs in Soto Zen as in other traditions. Meditators like to attend retreats or *sesshins* at the Throssel Hole Priory for concentrated meditation practice. There are blessings for babies, and marriages and funeral ceremonies. When Vajira buried one of her cats, the monks at Throssel Hole recited a funeral service

> with as much concern as for a person.

Every human is ordained a monk at his or her death, in the hope that rebirth will be conducive to enlightenment.

One feature of Zen Buddhism is the telling of stories, which are often the best way of getting a teaching across. I particularly liked one story which was told to me by one of Vajira's group:

> There was once a stonecutter who was working away cutting stone from a mountain. He was dissatisfied with his life and wished he could do something more important. One day a merchant came travelling by the mountain; he could buy and sell stone and other things and could travel the world. 'I wish I was that merchant,' said the stonecutter. It must have been a special day because his wish was instantly granted!
>
> At first he found the merchant's life exciting, but after a while travelling became tiring, especially when the sun was hot. The sun seemed to be the most powerful thing in the universe. 'I wish I was the sun,' said the ex-stonecutter, and yes, you've guessed, suddenly he was!
>
> He shone brightly down upon the land and was very happy until a cloud came along and blocked out his light. 'Clouds seem to be more powerful than the sun – I wish I was a cloud.'
>
> As a cloud he floated happily until he came to a mountain range. He could not pass over the mountain. The mountain was strong, unmovable. 'I wish I was a mountain.'
>
> As the mountain he stood tall and strong, but soon became aware of something chipping bits of him away. The mountain was powerless to do anything about it. He looked down and saw a stonecutter. 'I wish I was a stonecutter,' said he – and found himself back where he started. This time he decided to be content with what he was!

If you were wondering about Vajira's name, she was originally called Dorothy, which is a Christian name meaning 'gift of God', but was given the Buddhist name Vajira when she was ordained in the WBO before she found Soto Zen. Vajira means 'diamond', and Vajira feels that the associations of this name – strength, clarity and many-faceted – symbolise her practice of Buddhism.

When asked to sum up what Buddhism was about, Vajira said:

> The goal of Buddhism is enlightenment, full insight into things as they really are, the realisation that the Buddha nature is within all things. Buddhas are those who see this fully. Others have not yet woken up to this, and meditation is the way to wake up. There is no fixed point where your task is ended – 'you are always becoming Buddha' – but as you progress you understand more about the universe, and this has immediate practical benefits.

QUESTIONS

1 *What is it about Buddhism that would appeal to someone with a scientific training?*

2 *Vajira faces a blank wall when meditating. Why do you think she does this?*

3 *Why do Zen Buddhists consider it vital to have a personal teacher rather than just read about Buddhism in books?*

4 *Why is it important to be able to trace a line of teachers back to the Buddha?*

5 *Do you agree with Vajira that it is more important to work first at changing yourself rather than campaign to change the world?*

6 *What do you think Vajira's attitude would be to research involving experimentation on living animals (vivisection)?*

7 *Why do you think Vajira has artificial rather than real flowers on her shrine?*

8 *Can you guess what the bells, clappers and gong are used for?*

9 *What do you think is the point of having a statue of the Buddha, a picture of Roshi Kennett, candles and incense on an altar?*

10 *What do you think the story of the stonecutter is meant to teach?*

11 *What questions would you like to ask Vajira?*

2

REVEREND MASTER DAISHIN MORGAN:
serene reflection in a moorland setting (Soto Zen)

Talking to Vajira led me to arrange a visit to the place where she was ordained, Throssel Hole Priory, to see what Soto Zen was like in a monastic setting.

This involved a long journey to a remote hilltop, not far from Alston and the wild Pennine country around Cross Fell. In September sunshine it was a beautiful and peaceful scene, an ideal place for 'serene reflection' – but there was already a nip in the air. It must be very tough in winter. In fact on a previous attempt to visit the priory thick snow made the journey impossible.

The monks made us welcome with cups of tea and I met Reverend Master Daishin Morgan who is the Abbot in charge of the priory, his important status being shown by his brown robe and purple *kesa* or stole. Reverend Master Daishin Morgan has been a Buddhist monk since 1974. Before he became a Buddhist monk he worked for the Inland Revenue in London as a property valuer. I found his account of Buddhism very practical and down to earth. In fact, as with Vajira, it was the practical approach of Soto Zen Buddhism that first attracted him:

> I've always had an interest in religion and a desire for understanding. Buddhism offered a way, not an easy one, but at least the possibility of finding what I was looking for. It says enlightenment is possible and offers a practical and reasonable training for finding deeper truths.

He was also very impressed by the Buddhists that he met, especially Reverend Master Jiyu Kennett who became his teacher:

> No, my first meeting with my teacher was not an earthshattering cosmic experience, but she made a strong impression. I found her interesting and wanted to know more.

The most significant aspect of Buddhism for Reverend Master Daishin is the teaching on meditation. The 'serene reflection' (zazen) method taught in Soto Zen

> has helped me understand the teaching that all beings have the Buddha nature, the essence of enlightenment, compassion, love and wisdom. This realisation leads to a deep sense of reverence, of compassion and of gratitude.

Gratitude to whom, I wondered, having learned that Buddhism does not believe in God.

> There is something that is the object of the gratitude, but it is not a being in the sense of a personal God. It is something extremely undefined yet very close.

It is to this 'something' that the word Buddha refers.

> The Buddha is everywhere and in everything. Nothing is apart from Buddha nature. The Buddha nature is not something that exists inside of us like a soul, nor is it something external and apart from us like a god (or God). It is all of existence.

What Shakyamuni, the Buddha, realised is what is in all of us. This is something that is very difficult to talk about and must be directly experienced:

> The essence of Buddhahood is totally transcendent. We refer to it as 'the Unborn, the Undying, the Uncreated', that from which all things come; Truth, the eternal, the fabric of life, compassion, love and wisdom.

Meditation is the method by which this Buddha nature can be experienced. The point of meditation is

> to know who you are, to find out what the real basis of life is, and from that to find the true source of action.

Realising that you are not separate from the eternal enables you to accept yourself as you are, including the negative side, and to become a less selfish person:

> You become a pipe for the compassion of the eternal.

From the Throssel Hole Priory publication *Serene Reflection Meditation*, I learned that zazen meditation consists of sitting in a meditation position, with eyes open, in a suitable place without distractions (e.g. in front of a blank wall), letting thoughts arise, but letting them go rather than grasping them. It is described as 'neither trying to think nor trying not to think'. It is recommended as a daily practice for a period up to about 40 minutes.

How does meditation fit into the daily routine of the priory? For about 200 days of the year the community is in full training. This means getting up at 5 a.m., then half an hour's meditation, morning service and perhaps half an hour of chores before breakfast at 7.30.

The monks eat meals in a formal manner in the meditation hall. Each monk has a 2 m by 1 m space and a cupboard in the wall. For the first seven years of training you eat, sleep and meditate in that space. This means that you learn to be very thoughtful about the others sharing the room.

After breakfast there is a reading period, from 8.00 to 8.30, when monks read the *Kyojukaimon*, a commentary on the Buddhist precepts by Roshi Kennett. From 8.30 to 1 p.m. there is work – cleaning, cooking, gardening, building work or whatever needs to be done, with a short break for tea. Lunch is at 1 p.m. and after a short rest period there is an hour's work from 2.15 to 3.15. At 3.30 there is a brief 'midday' service followed by half an hour of meditation. A simple supper takes place at 6.00 and this is followed by a period of quiet reflection. From 8.00 there is communal meditation, until 8.45 which is time for tea and socialising. I was surprised to find that the monks watched television and videos, and not just serious programmes but comedies and soap operas:

> It stops us getting out of touch with ordinary people.

Lights out in the zendo or meditation hall is at 10 p.m.

Outside the 200 days the monks rise an hour later, at 6 a.m., except on Mondays when there is a sleep-in until 7.30. Sunday afternoons are a time for rest, and Sunday evenings are for relaxation:

> We might watch something like *Star Wars*.

Anyone joining the community of monks will have taken jukai or lay ordination, like Vajira, and spent a period of between six months and a few years as a postulant trying out the monastic life. The ordination ceremony is similar to that for lay people, but also involves having the head shaved and receiving the robe, bowl and mat. Monks do not follow the 227 rules of the *Vinaya* as Theravada monks do, but observe the Ten Precepts listed in the first interview plus some basic rules regulating life in the monastery. They do eat after midday; supper is called the 'medicine meal', a practice introduced when Buddhism moved from India to colder climates. One of the Zen rules is the opposite to that for Theravada monks:

> A day without work is a day without food.

In Japan monks can be married, but the Western tradition found that this caused difficulties and now all monks remain single. Women can become monks too, and there is no distinction at all made between the sexes (hence women are called monks rather than nuns). Junior monks wear a black robe and kesa, more senior monks wear a black robe and a yellow kesa, and monks with over seven years' training wear a brown robe and purple kesa. At this stage a monk is able to teach others. The robe and the shaved head tell other people what you are, and remind you yourself what you have to live up to. Monks are allowed to wear ordinary clothes in a situation where the robes might cause difficulties.

Monks are allowed one week's holiday every year to visit family and friends, and families are welcome to visit at any time:

> You still love your family of course.

The priory as a building consists of the zendo or meditation hall, the ceremony hall (which is also the lay meditation hall), the kitchen, private rooms for senior monks, the dining room and a room with chairs for talks. Traditionally, a monastery is laid out in the shape of a human being, with the ceremony hall as the head and the zendo as the heart. The 'head' would face north towards the Pole Star, which in Chinese tradition is the unmoving centre of the universe. The 'left arm' would be the bathhouse and the 'right arm' the toolshed. However, this traditional layout is not found at Throssel Hole as the priory was not purpose-built.

The zendo and ceremony hall are quiet and peaceful. There is a large altar in the ceremony hall where offerings of flowers, fruit, water, light and incense are made before a large statue of the Buddha. There are also images of bodhisattvas, such as *Kwannon* (also called in Chinese *Kwanyin*). This female figure, sometimes misleadingly referred to as 'the goddess of mercy', embodies the infinite compassion of the Buddha nature, also represented in male form as *Kanzeon* (Indian name: *Avalokitesvara*).

In the zendo for the monks there is a large stature of bodhisattva *Manjusri* seated on a lion which has big, doleful eyes. Manjusri represents enlightened wisdom and the lion the untamed self, which is not really separate from the eternal but thinks it is. A bodhisattva is a being dedicated to enlightenment and seeking the salvation of all beings. All Zen Buddhists are trying to follow the bodhisattva path.

The zendo is the place where monks meditate, sleep and eat. Meals are taken in silence. Everything is done with great mindfulness and concentration. Reverence must be shown to the food, to the utensils and to those offering the food. Everything must be handled gently, remembering all the hard work and natural resources that have gone into bringing this food to you. Greed for food should be put aside, remembering that you eat not to satisfy your cravings, but simply to stay alive. Scriptures are recited at the beginning of the meal to remind all those taking part that something as ordinary and everyday as eating can be turned into a form of meditation.

At Throssel Hole food is vegetarian but cheese, eggs and milk are eaten. If a monk were invited to a meal and given meat, he or she would eat it for

> after all, if it is already dead, it is disrespectful not to use that death for a good purpose.

The monk might later point out tactfully that vegetarian food is preferred. The basic idea is to do as little harm as possible:

> Killing vegetables is still killing, but better than killing animals. We must recognise that we all take life to live and should therefore put our lives to the best use we can.

In Japan, Buddhists do drink alcohol, but members of the Soto Zen tradition in the UK would rarely do so.

In general, ethical questions are left to the individual conscience. The Ten Precepts (see p. 18) give guidelines and rule out killing, stealing, lying and so on. However, more important than lists of do's and don'ts are the overriding precepts:

> Cease from evil, do only good and do good for others.

In every situation the Buddhist should decide which course of action does least harm and most good. This means that Buddhists might disagree on questions such as whether or not there should be nuclear weapons. One issue that Reverend Master Morgan felt strongly about was capital punishment:

> Buddhism teaches respect for life, and the teaching on rebirth shows that death does not end the problem.

Abortion, he feels, is fundamentally wrong, but to ban it might lead to worse harm. Caring for the environment has a high priority for Buddhists, who believe that all things are connected, and that the Buddha nature is in all things. Sexuality is one area where Soto Zen Buddhist opinion might differ from that of non-Buddhists:

> Essentially the ideal is celibacy. It is not considered freakish to be celibate. Sexual activity is not, however, seen as a sin, but sexual

self-indulgence is seen as contrary to the precepts. Certainly it would not be appropriate in a monastery.

The priory calendar marks 31 special days celebrating the life of the Buddha, important bodhisattvas and great teachers from the past, together with the autumn and spring equinoxes. In Mahayana Buddhism the Buddha's birth, enlightenment and death are celebrated separately. Buddha's birthday is celebrated on 8 May and is a special time for children. A statue of the newly born Buddha is placed in a fountain of water and people ladle water over the statue. The fountain is a symbol of overflowing love, and ladling the water is a prayer that you will find the source of compassion within yourself as the Buddha did. Children make lotus blossoms out of paper and decorate the room. Buddha's passing is celebrated on 15 February, and his enlightenment on 25 December. In Japan the latter would be on 8 December, but it has been altered in Britain to coincide with Christmas, which is also a festival of light coming into the world.

New Year (1 January rather than Chinese New Year) is important as a new start. On 31 October the dead are remembered at the festival of 'feeding the hungry ghosts'. The phrase 'hungry ghosts' translates the Indian word *preta*, which is one of the traditional forms into which beings can be reborn – in addition to humans, animals, gods, demons (or 'jealous gods') and beings in hells. In Chinese tradition, this festival is celebrated earlier in October, but the date of 31 October fits in well with Christian remembrance of the dead on Halloween, All Saints' Day and All Souls' Day, and also with the Celtic festival of the dead, the New Year Samhain. It is also suitably near 'bonfire night' (itself probably a development of Samhain), because at the festival of 'hungry ghosts' a bonfire or ceremonial pyre is lit. Paper ihais, small funeral plaques are burned on the fire, to wish dead relatives well on their journey. Any hindrances from which release is sought – such as anger or resentment – can be symbolically thrown away by writing them down too and throwing them on the fire. Although the Halloween date is suitable, the priory is thinking of celebrating this festival earlier in future, on 21 September. This is also a traditional time in Japan for remembering the dead. By 31 October it is getting pretty cold up on the Pennines for an outdoor celebration!

As a monk, Reverend Daishin Morgan is involved in performing ceremonies for lay people as well as teaching. There is a special service for naming babies, where the baby is sprinkled with water and offered to the protection of the buddhas and ancestors. A special wedding ceremony has been devised which combines Buddhist and British traditions. In many forms of Buddhism there is no wedding ceremony, but it was introduced in Japan by a fourteenth-century Soto Zen teacher. As well as exchanging rings in the British custom, each partner holds a candle and they then symbolically light one large candle between them and blow out their separate candles. Their hands are bound together with the Buddhist rosary (prayer beads) and a marriage contract is signed. Their life together is dedicated to working for the good of all beings. In Japan the modern custom is to wear white, but in the UK people tend to wear their best clothes.

However, as in all forms of Buddhism, in Soto Zen death is the most significant part of the life cycle:

> Death is seen as an opportunity to let go of clinging, hatred and delusion and become one with the eternal.

The dead are laid out as if for ordination, with shaved head, rosary, ketchimyaku and kesa. The coffin is placed on the altar in the place of the Buddha statue to symbolise that the dead person *is* Buddha. The *Three Refuges* and Ten Precepts are recited as in an ordination ceremony. The funeral service emphasises the need for the mourners to let go of their loved one at death. The body may be cremated or buried; there is a cemetery at Throssel Hole. There may be an all-night vigil the night before the funeral. The mourners are encouraged to participate in the services and will offer incense, carry the funeral plaque, flowers and other ceremonial requisites, and help to fill in the grave. The monk conducting the funeral will talk to the relatives about death and what it means. Reverend Master Daishin Morgan and other monks travel all over the country to perform funeral ceremonies. Small ihais are kept in the ceremony hall.

So what happens to people when they die?

> At death a being returns to the 'great ocean' of the eternal, but if there is any selfish clinging remaining this needs a way to sort itself out and that leads to rebirth. It is not personal rebirth in the sense of one continuing entity dying here and being reborn there. Rather it is that which is left that needs to be cleansed. Rebirth is not punishment but an opportunity for working out whatever still needs to be worked out. For example, a person with tremendous lust to sort out may be reborn as an animal, or someone too attached to a particular place might become a sort of ghostly manifestation there, or if you have hated a lot you will encounter a lot of hate.

How do you know that rebirth is true?

> Through meditation you can recall previous lives. Not in the sense of whole life histories, full names and dates etc., not 'I was Napoleon',

but flashes of memory, usually related to a problem you are working on. Often it is a painful memory, perhaps of being rejected or even killed. It helps you understand why you are what you are now.

Such memories usually come to those who have been training for some time rather than to the beginner. Reverend Master Daishin accepts that other people could have different explanations for these experiences.

Meditation also helps one cope with death. Death should not be feared because

> There is but one great life. Therefore whatever happens that life is eternal. Life is life, death is death and there is no need to fear either. In order to meditate completely you have to let yourself go and that is what death is, what we fear about death. So through meditation you lose the fear of death and are set free to live.

This understanding of death means that you can help others to face death. As well as conducting funerals, monks spend time helping the dying and the bereaved. While I spent several hours talking to Reverend Master Daishin Morgan, the young guest master gave up his free Sunday afternoon to talk to my parents who had very recently been bereaved. He also made them lots of cups of tea.

QUESTIONS

1 *Why do you think such a remote place was chosen for the Soto Zen training monastery?*

2 *Why do you think meditation is one of the greatest attractions in Buddhism?*

3 *How near is the Zen idea of 'Buddha' to the idea of 'God' in other religions?*

4 *Why do you think you are advised to keep your eyes open in zazen meditation?*

5 *Why do you think the decision was made that monks should not marry?*

6 *Many Buddhists do not have religious ceremonies for marriages. Why do you think the Soto Zen tradition has developed a wedding service?*

7 *Why are funerals considered more important than naming babies or weddings?*

8 *How does meditation help people to cope with death?*

9 *Why do you think ihais are kept in shrine rooms?*

10 *If you could ask Reverend Daishin Morgan a further question, what would it be?*

3

KHEMADHAMMO THERO:
the Forest Hermitage (Theravada)

Khemadhammo Thero looks like most people's idea of a typical Buddhist. He is a monk with a shaved head and a brownish-yellow robe, who lives in an ivy-covered house with a lovely, peaceful garden in the middle of a forest in Warwickshire. He talks quietly and gently, and he laughs a lot. The 'Forest Hermitage' feels very calm and peaceful. Khemadhammo (his name means something like 'secure peace') is a *thero* or senior monk of at least ten years' standing and an *ajahn* or Buddhist teacher. He belongs to a strict forest-dwelling tradition taught by Ajahn Chah in Wat Pah Pong in North-East Thailand.

Khemadhammo went to drama school and spent several years as an actor before becoming interested in Buddhism. He was attracted by meditation and decided to go to Thailand to train seriously with a teacher. Ajahn Chah insists on a five-year commitment. When asked what attracted him, Khemadhammo replied:

> Buddhism is not so much a religion as a practical way of improving oneself. It is all up to you. The Buddhist teaching of karma means that it is your own actions that bring you happiness or suffering. You have to take responsibility for yourself.

Khemadhammo was ordained in Thailand as a *samanera* in December 1971 and a *bhikkhu* in May 1972. A samanera is a 'little monk' or 'novice', and you have to be a samanera first. Even very small boys can be samaneras, but to be a bhikkhu you have to be at least 20 years old. The ordination ceremony involves the presence of five other monks and takes place within the *sima* or monastery boundary. You must have your parents' permission and no responsibilities like debt or national service. The candidate has his head shaved, and receives the robe, a new name to symbolise a new life and the few possessions that a monk is allowed. These include the alms bowl, a razor, needle and thread, water strainer, fan, umbrella and candles. The robe of a forest monk is brownish-yellow whereas other Theravada monks wear bright orange. It consists of three sections:

> The robe is a symbol of renouncing luxury. It is cut and sewn to

resemble patchwork, because the original robes were made from scrap rags. It is also very practical even if it doesn't look it! I think that it is important for people to be able to identify you as a Buddhist monk by what you wear.

Theravada monks live a very strict life. They keep the Five Moral Precepts which apply to all Theravada Buddhists (see p. 42). They also keep many more rules: altogether there are 227 precepts making up the basic rule known as the *Patimokkha*, contained in the Vinaya section of the Pali Canon. These rules include not eating after midday, not wearing jewellery, not attending amusements like dances, not having a luxurious bed and never handling money. Forest monks often practise an even stricter lifestyle, for example having only one meal a day. Monks by definition are celibate and several of the rules make sure that this is not a problem: for example, as a woman I was not allowed to speak to Khemadhammo without a chaperon. This avoids any possible gossip or scandal; a monk must always be a good example to others. Theravada monks cannot grow food or cook for themselves, but rely on others to provide food. In Thailand and sometimes in Britain this means going out on an alms round, but in the latter case it is often more practical for supporters to bring food to the monastery.

Life in a monastery in Thailand is strictly regulated. The day begins very early, the monks rising at about 2.30 a.m. Chanting is followed by the alms round in a nearby village, the mid-morning meal, meditation, chores, evening chanting and meditation in one's own hut until quite late. In Britain the day can be varied, but there is still morning and evening chanting in the shrine at about 7 a.m. and 8 p.m., the one meal a day and periods of meditation.

> Study of scripture does not play a big part in the forest tradition. Of course the teachings and rules come from the Pali Canon, but scripture is not the same as practical experience.

A variety of meditations are practised, such as concentration on breathing, analysis of the body and mind, and meditation on loving kindness:

> The point of meditation is to gain insight into the truth about life, to learn awareness and control of the mind.

Meditation helps you to see into the meaning of Buddhist teachings which have practical results. For Khemadhammo

> the most liberating teaching of Buddhism is that of anatta or 'no self'.

It may seem a difficult idea as it challenges our normal obsessions with ourselves, but it frees us from worrying about ourselves all the time.

Buddhism teaches that there is no permanent, unchanging inner 'me', only changing feelings, thoughts and physical components. Meditation helps you realise this as you observe and become more aware of your body and mind:

Realising this means we can learn to do things for their own sake, without worry or selfishness, without the sense of self intruding.

Khemadhammo does not spend all his time in the hermitage. He visits prisons as a Buddhist chaplain as part of an organisation which hopes to provide Buddhist chaplains for all prisons. He teaches meditation to prisoners who request it, as well as offering counselling:

Prison is a painful and lonely experience. For some people it may be the first time they ever sat still or reflected upon their lives and so meditation can offer a skill which turns this into a positive experience. However, prisons are not peaceful places like monasteries, they are noisy, violent and harsh. For some prisoners it is hard to do much.

Buddhism teaches caring and compassion for all living things. Khemadhammo prefers to eat vegetarian food because the killing of animals for food seems to go against the 'non-harming' principle of Buddhism. However, the rules allow you to eat meat that has not been specially killed for you. In Thailand, Buddhists do eat meat:

The scriptures are ambiguous on this. The Buddha did not want this to be a problematic issue. However, non-harming seems to me to rule out meat eating.

For Khemadhammo, Buddhism gives clear guidelines on most controversial moral issues:

There is no possible justification for war or nuclear weapons. They bring suffering even when not used, because of the worry about them. The deterrence argument is nonsense as to be a real deterrent you have to be prepared to use them, which is just so immoral.

Life begins in the womb, so an abortion is killing, tantamount to murder.

Smoking is unhealthy, but not a strong drug like alcohol. It is not really important as it only affects your body not your mind. Some monks do smoke. Alcohol and drugs affect your mind and self-control and are therefore not allowed by the Buddhist precepts.

Every morning and evening Khemadhammo will chant in Pali from a book of Buddhist worship. Lay people attend the evening chanting at 8 p.m. on Mondays and Fridays. Khemadhammo will also guide people through a meditation session in the shrine room. The shrine room contains a large golden Buddha. People will bow to the statue and praise the Buddha in words, but even uneducated peasants in Thailand laugh at the idea that they are worshipping an idol:

> You are not paying respects to the image but to the ideal of enlightenment which the image represents. The Buddha is not a god to contact and ask for favours.

There are ceremonies and festivals in Buddhism but they are not very important and offer cultural rather than religious customs:

> Buddha was not keen on ceremonies.

In Thailand monks may bless a baby or a couple after marriage. They will chant sections of the scriptures which have protective power, but the real power is the teaching itself. Young men often spend a brief period as monks around the age of 20. This is a Thai custom which Khemadhammo thinks is a good thing:

> It means that most of the male population understand what the monastic life is about. It is a marvellous opportunity if used properly.

Buddhist monks do not conduct marriages but they do conduct funerals, which are cremations.

Theravada Buddhists celebrate four main festivals, which are named after the months in which they occur. *Wesak* on the full moon of May celebrates the birth, enlightenment and passing of the Buddha. *Asala* in July celebrates his first sermon. The *Vassa* or rainy season retreat starts the day after *Asala*. This is very important for monks. They do less travelling and make special efforts in their practice. Some time after the end of Vassa in October the *Kathina* ceremony is arranged. A special robe is presented to the sangha by the lay people, which is then given to the most deserving monk. They also bring robes, presents and a *dana* or food offering for the monastery. Monks will visit each other's monasteries for this ceremony:

> It sometimes gets embarrassing as so many people, especially from Asian Buddhist countries, want to offer the Kathina robe and provide the food. It is a big day for both the sangha and the lay people.

Magha Puja in February is the Thai festival which commemorates a huge spontaneous gathering of enlightened monks, all personally ordained by the Buddha, at which he gave some important guiding principles and asked that they should be heard regularly at meetings of the sangha. These included 'avoid all evil, cultivate the good, and purify the mind'. The Buddha made rules only when they were needed and it was many years before more precise rules were required.

When asked to sum up what Buddhism was about, Khemadhammo said:

> The aim of Buddhism is to know from your own experience what the Buddha knows. The meaning of Buddha is one who knows. And what does he know? That in our ordinary life things are impermanent, inherently unsatisfactory and without self, coming and going dependent on conditions.

The aspects of experience that Khemadhammo picked out refer to the basic teachings of Buddhism, summed up in the Four Noble Truths and the Three Marks of Life. Buddhism is really about the problem of life and how to solve it. Life as we experience it is a terrible mystery: there is suffering and unsatisfactoriness (dukkha), nothing lasts (anicca) and even people change and die (anatta):

> The Buddha did repeatedly state that all he taught, all he was really interested in, was dukkha and the end or stopping of dukkha.

The whole point and purpose of the monastic life is to share the Buddha's knowledge of suffering, its cause and its solution; and like the Buddha to discover happiness and peace and to help others do the same.

QUESTIONS

1 *Why do you think some Buddhist monks choose to live in forest retreats?*

2 *Why do you think monks shave their heads?*

3 *Why do they renounce all luxuries and possess only the bare necessities of life?*

4 *Why do you think Theravada monks place a fan in front of their face when chanting the Buddhist scriptures?*

5 *What advantages and disadvantages can you see in the practice of wearing the robe and shaving the head?*

6 *Why do you think Buddhist monks choose to live an unmarried life, with no family or paid employment?*

7 *Why do you think the Buddha's original simple moral guidelines had to be developed into more detailed rules?*

8 *How would it affect both monks and lay supporters that monks are reliant on others for their food?*

9 *Why do you think Theravada forest monks spend more time meditating than studying scriptures?*

10 *Why do you think some people become Buddhists while in prison?*

11 *Why do you think Khemadhammo considers visiting prisoners an important task?*

12 *Why does Khemadhammo consider both nuclear weapons and abortion to be totally immoral? Do you think all Buddhists would agree with him?*

13 *Do you agree that alcohol is a more harmful drug than cigarettes?*

14 *If Buddha is not a god, and his image is a symbol, why do you think Buddhists have images, candles, flowers, water and incense on their shrines?*

15 *Why do you think births and marriages are not considered to be very important as religious celebrations in this tradition of Buddhism, whereas funerals are considered important and are conducted by Buddhist monks?*

16 *Do you think that it is a good idea for young men to spend some time in a monastery as in the Thai tradition? Can you see any disadvantages? Do you think it would be a good idea for young women too?*

17 *Why do you think lay people enjoy the festivals and welcome the opportunity of being able to provide food and robes for the monks?*

18 *Hermit monks have sometimes been accused of being interested only in their own salvation. After reading about Khemadhammo, do you think this accusation is true?*

19 *If you could ask Khemadhammo a further question, what would it be?*

4

THE GOONEWARDENE FAMILY:
a Sri Lankan family in Britain (Theravada)

The Goonewardene family live in North London and made me very welcome on my visit to their home. I was invited to lunch and shared a delicious meal of traditional Sri Lankan food: rice, several different curries and sambol which is hot savoury coconut. It brought back memories for me as I once spent a month in Sri Lanka and soon developed a taste for chillis in everything and curry for breakfast, lunch and dinner. I was surprised to find that both in Sri Lanka and in Britain many Sri Lankan Buddhists eat meat. In the Goonewardene family, Mrs Goonewardene and one of the three boys are vegetarian, but her husband and the two other boys are not.

The general opinion common in Sri Lanka, based on what the Buddha himself said, is that

> You can eat meat if you haven't actually killed the animal yourself.

However, like many Buddhists who eat meat, the family are aware of a clash here with basic Buddhist principles. Chula, the eldest boy, said:

> If you buy meat, it has been killed for you really.

It is something for people to make their own minds up about:

> It is hard to give up meat if you have been brought up to eat it.
> Can children be healthy on a vegetarian diet?

As seven-year-old Rahal commented:

> I don't really like eating meat because it means killing animals, but I don't really like vegetables!

As a result of this problem over meat eating I found that the butchers in Sri Lanka tended to be of other religions. Many Buddhists were prepared to eat meat but few were prepared actually to kill the animals.

The Goonewardene family are Anil (Mr Goonewardene), Sunethra (Mrs Goonewardene) and their three boys Chula, Manoj and Rahal, who when I met them in 1987 were aged 13, 10 and 7. Mr and Mrs Goonewardene were born in Sri Lanka and have lived in Britain since 1960 and 1970 respectively. The boys were all born in Britain and have never been to Sri Lanka; their accents and interests are the same as other North London boys. All three were full of life, especially little Rahal, and they enjoyed telling me all their favourite jokes as well as all about Buddhism.

Mr Anil Goonewardene lectures in Law at a polytechnic. Both Anil and Sunethra come from families which have been Buddhist for generations and which have been involved in Buddhist work. Sunethra's father donated the land for and built the Talawakelle temple in Sri Lanka. Mrs Goonewardene has impaired sight and owns a lively guide dog. She says:

> When you are born into a Buddhist family you will be guided by Buddhist teaching. There is no particular ceremony for becoming a Buddhist, although babies may be taken to the temple for a blessing. We took the children to Chiswick *Vihara* when they were born and the monks chanted sections of the Buddhist scriptures as a sort of blessing. It is not a magic ceremony to ensure good fortune; it is really the power of thought and the value of the Buddha's teaching.

The nearest there is to a ceremony of initiation into Buddhism is the reciting by all Buddhists of what are known as the Three Refuges:

I take refuge in the Buddha.
I take refuge in the *Dhamma*.
I take refuge in the Sangha.

In other words they commit themselves to the Enlightened One, his teaching and the community which preserves his teaching. In addition they will recite the Five Precepts (see below) and make a conscious effort to observe them. Both adults and children agree that the most valuable thing about a Buddhist upbringing is that

> It gives you a sense of belonging, a clear way of life and a moral code to live by.

The five precepts undertaken by all Theravada lay people and recited regularly with the three refuges are as follows:

1 To refrain from killing
2 To refrain from stealing (taking what is not given)
3 To avoid bad conduct in sensual matters
4 To refrain from lying and swearing
5 To refrain from drugs and alcoholic drinks.

According to Chula, the Five Precepts are the basic moral values on which most people, whether Buddhist or not, would agree. One difference is that Buddhists are less likely to be cruel to animals. Seven-year-old Rahal has seen children

> stamping on insects and shooting animals. What I like best about Buddhism is that we do not hurt animals.

The Buddhist moral code is not an inflexible list of rules to be followed. It does not tell you what to do in every circumstance but is meant to make you think more carefully about what you are doing, and work out for yourself whether it is the most wise, kind and 'skilful' course of action. In practice, morality can be difficult. Chula's current difficulties concern going fishing. On the one hand Buddhism teaches kindness to animals. On the other hand he likes to go fishing with his friends. Do fish feel pain? Is it all right if the fish are always thrown back alive? It is up to Chula to decide what he should do according to Buddhist teachings:

> Buddhism teaches that you shouldn't do things just because it is the fashion to do so, or because others are doing it, or because people tell you to. You should do what is right.

Fishing is obviously an important issue for young Buddhists. In an edition of *Rainbows*, a magazine for Theravada Buddhist children produced by Amaravati Buddhist centre, there was an article about fishing. It did not tell children not to fish, but asked them to reflect on the suffering of fish and the greed that leads fish to be caught, and then to decide whether or not they should go fishing.

Other decisions in the moral area can also be difficult. Buddhist precepts teach that you must not 'take what is not given'.

> If you find £5 and keep it, is it stealing?

ask Chula. He thinks not, but his mother thinks it is. Buddhism teaches that the most important thing in a moral action is your intention. If you think that you are doing the wisest, kindest thing then that is what matters.

Do the parents drink alcohol? A little, occasionally. The children giggle at this.

In this country, where Buddhists are a small minority, it is not easy to ensure that children receive a Buddhist upbringing. At school, Chula cannot remember having much religious education. At primary school it was mostly Christian – Bible stories, the geography of

Israel and celebrating Christmas. At secondary school religion is not talked about much. You are more likely to be teased for the colour of your skin than for your religion. However,

> Once at school children from different religons spoke about their faiths. There were more different religions than I had imagined, and more people were willing to stand up and talk about their beliefs than I would have expected.

From the parents' point of view,

> Buddhist parents are very keen that the children acquire a good Buddhist background.

It is important that children know about Buddhism and about their cultural heritage; the two are often tied up together. The children attend Sunday school for one or two hours every fortnight. This is held at the Chiswick Vihara, a Theravada temple with monks who are mainly Sinhalese (from Sri Lanka). Anil teaches at this school. All the teaching is done on a voluntary basis and, as is customary for a temple, no charge is made for the teaching. The children learn the life story of the Buddha, the Buddhist moral precepts and how to put these into practice, and basic Buddhist teachings taken from the scriptures but expressed in simple terms by monks and lay teachers. The children's favourite sections of the scripture are the *Jataka* tales, stories in the form of fables about previous lives of the Buddha before be became a buddha. These stores illustrate how a good Buddhist should behave. Most often they stress self-sacrificing love.

I asked the children to tell me their favourite stories from either the life of the Buddha or the Jataka tales. Rahal's story comes from the life of the Buddha:

> When Prince Siddhartha was a boy his cousin shot a swan. It landed at Siddhartha's feet. He took the arrow out and put ointment on the wound and made it better. His cousin asked, 'Do you know where my swan is? Oh, you've got it, give it back to me.' Siddhartha said, 'No, it's mine, it landed at my feet.' His cousin replied, 'It's mine! I shot it with my bow.' They began to argue. Siddhartha suggested that they should go to court like grown-ups do when they argue. They asked the wise men of Siddhartha's father's court. Some took Siddhartha's side, others took his cousin's side. The wisest man of all made the final decision. 'It belongs to the one who was trying to help it, not the one who tried to hurt it. All living creatures want to live and be happy, so we have no right to hurt them.'

Manoj chose a Jataka story, about a monkey king:

> Once upon a time in India mangoes were very rare. A tribe of monkeys were living in some trees by a river. Downriver there was a town, but the people there did not know about the monkeys or the mangoes that grew in their trees. The wise king of the monkeys told the monkeys not to let any mangoes fall in the water, otherwise they would be carried downstream to the town. The men would find the mangoes and come upstream looking for mangoes, and would find and attack the monkeys. However, eventually one mango fell in the river and was found by a fisherman. Men came upstream from the town to find the rare mangoes and started shooting at the monkeys. The monkey king tried to make a bridge across the river so that the monkeys could escape from the men. He had a rope but found it was not quite long enough to reach the trees on the other side. He attached the rope to his feet and found he could reach the trees with his hands. He called to the monkeys to cross the river using himself as part of the bridge. The monkeys ran across to safety, but the monkey king's back was broken. He fell to the ground. The king of the humans noticed this and went over to the dying monkey king. He praised his devotion to his people, looked after the monkey until he died, and tried always to be as kind a leader of his people as the monkey king was of his.

Chula's story was about a rabbit:

> Once upon a time there were a rabbit, a donkey, a kingfisher and a jackal. Their custom was to collect food in the morning and eat it together in the afternoon. A man came walking through the forest dressed as tramp, and starving with hunger. He asked each of the animals in turn for some food. The jackal gave him some meat, the kingfisher gave him some fish, and the donkey gave him some fruit. But rabbits eat grass and humans cannot eat grass. The rabbit wanted to help the man and stop him dying of hunger. He told the man to build a fire. 'I will jump over it until the heat kills me and then you can roast and eat me.' The tramp stopped him and revealed that he was really a king in disguise who had come to test the rabbit's kindness. This story is to teach us the importance of being generous and putting others before ourselves.

The children can sit a course of examinations in Buddhism which are set in Sri Lanka by the Young Men's Buddhist Association. Chula has passed the senior-level and Manoj the preliminary-level examination. Most of the children who attend the Sunday school are from Sri Lankan families, but there are also some children from English Buddhist families.

Buddhist families also perform Buddhist rituals and ceremonies. Most will have a statue of the Buddha in their homes, possibly in a special shrine. Some families perform daily *puja* or worship which includes offerings of flowers, incense, candles and food to the Buddha statue and repeating in Pali the Three Refuges and the Five Precepts. This is not worshipping an idol as the statue is just there as a reminder of the Buddha and his teaching. It is not like praying to God:

We don't know where he is. He cannot hear you or answer prayers.

The offerings are made to show respect to the man and his teachings,

to say thank you to the Buddha for bringing the teachings.

There are also symbols that remind people of the Buddha's teachings. There are Pali phrases that explain the offerings. Flowers fade, reminding you that all things, including yourself, will not last for ever. Incense reminds you of the sweetness of the Buddha's way of life. Candles remind you that his teachings light up the darkness of ignorance. Food reminds you of the importance of helping others, especially the poor and the hungry.

The Goonewardene family keep their Buddha statues on a high shelf but do not practise daily puja together. The boys will take flowers to offer at the shrine in the Chiswick Vihara where the monks will chant the Three Refuges and Five Precepts in Pali for the children to repeat. They do not visit the vihara as a family every week, but will go to the temple on special occasions. This will involve puja, listening to the monks chanting –

this has a beneficial effect of calming the mind

listening to a talk by one of the monks and perhaps talking to the monks informally.

On special occasions, families will either visit the vihara or invite the monks to their house for a 'blessing'. This means that the family will provide dana or a meal for the monks, and the monks will chant *pirit* or special sections of the Buddhist scriptures. Such occasions might include a birth, a marriage, moving to a new house, going into hospital or taking an important examination. Marriages are civil, with no special religious ceremony, but a blessing is often requested afterwards. What does a blessing do for you?

It is not magic, it is the effect on your own mind that is important.

In a way,

> It may not accord with strict Buddhist teaching [that only moral actions and not rituals affect your future]; it is a social custom.

A blessing is an expression of goodwill and many Buddhists feel it is beneficial to the recipient.

There is a religious ceremony involving the monks for funerals. In a Sri Lankan village a funeral pyre is made with wood. A close relative such as a son or grandson will light the fire after walking around the pyre three times. The monks and the family may chant pirit all night. Three days after the funeral, seven days after, three months after and on every anniversary, meals will be given to the monks and to the poor and pirit will be chanted. Water is poured out to symbolise that the *merit* of the ceremony is passed on to the dead relative.

The Goonewardene family attend temple for Buddhist festivals. Sri Lankan Buddhist festivals include Wesak in May, which celebrates the Buddha's birth, enlightenment and death, *Poson* in June, which celebrates the first preaching of Buddhism in Sri Lanka, and Asala in July, which celebrates the Buddha's first sermon. They also attend temple for Sinhalese New Year, just after Easter, which is not really a religious festival. This shows how religion and culture are often closely tied together.

> At New Year we have presents for the classes, maybe a book or a Buddha statue made by the monks. We also eat special food such as milk-rice which is prepared for special days like festivals and birthdays, light candles and incense and can spend our pocket money.

At Wesak and other festivals some Buddhists take Ten Precepts for the day. This means adding the following to the Five Precepts:

6 No food after midday
7 No luxurious bed (sleeping on a mat)
8 No jewellery, perfume, make-up or fancy clothes
9 No amusements like dancing or shows
10 No money

Sometimes these are known as the *Eight Precepts*, by omitting number 10 and putting 8 and 9 together.

The celebration of a festival means a whole day of Buddhist activities at the temple. There will be a programme of lectures, discussions and sermons. Dana is prepared for the monks who eat before twelve noon and then the lay people have a communal meal.

People often wear white for festivals. At Wesak in Sri Lanka,

> The roads are lit up with women carrying candles and making music with drums. The temples are decorated and there may be a procession of the people around the neighbouring area, starting and finishing at the temple. There is a continual chanting of pirit and a bustle of people coming and going. Often the supporters of the temple set up a 'dansala' where food is provided free for anyone who comes in. People also light up their homes with lanterns and oil lamps. The village may set up a 'pandol', which is a scene from the life of the Buddha made from wood and paper and lit up from behind. Cards are sent, but this is really a modern custom copied from Western countries.

Poson is a more purely religious occasion when people will take the Ten Precepts and devote the day to religious activity.

Pilgrimages are enjoyed by Buddhists. In India people will visit the sites associated with the Buddha: the places of his birth, his death, his first sermon and his enlightenment, and the towns in which he stayed. Not many Sri Lankans travel to India, however, and there are several places of pilgrimage on the island of Sri Lanka which are associated with a legendary visit there by the Buddha. A favourite pilgrimage is to climb the mountain known as Sri Pada, where it is said that you can see the Buddha's footprint. Chula is sceptical:

> They've just made it up.

His mother replies:

> It's the thought that counts.

Other places include the Bo-tree at the ancient town of Anuradha-pura, said to have grown from a cutting from the original tree under which the Buddha sat. There is also a temple at Kandy which houses the Buddha's tooth relic. Once a year in August there is a series of processions lasting a fortnight in honour of this relic. This 'perahera' is a great attraction for Buddhists and tourists alike as it involves colourfully attired dancers, drummers and elephants.

The nearest thing to a pilgrimage in Britain is a visit to a large Buddhist vihara like Amaravati near Hemel Hempstead. The children enjoy these visits which take place several times a year at holiday seasons. Rahal's favourite monk is Ajahn Sumedho, the Abbot,

> because he laughs a lot and likes children.

Amaravati has a special room for children, the Rainbow Room.

> We hear stories and play games. Once we collected leaves outside and a nun showed us a leaf from the Bo-tree. Once we found a monk in a hut in the garden!

According to Mr Goonewardene,

> Buddhists like to visit all kinds of holy places including those of other religions, and will enter such premises with the greatest respect and reverence.

Tolerance of other faiths seem to be an important characteristic of Buddhism. On occasions such as these visits to Amaravati, the family will take dana or food for the monks and the children will help put the food in the monks' bowls:

> It is altogether a happy and joyful occasion.

Many British converts to Buddhism talk about meditation as one of the main attractions of the religion. Buddhist monks and nuns spend long periods in meditation, especially those of the 'forest-dwelling' tradition. The Goonewardene family, like many people from Buddhist countries, did not talk much about meditation. I received the impression that it was not as important for them as living a moral life. However, Mr Goonewardene commented that

> The word 'meditation' is a poor translation of the Pali word *bhavana*, which means 'mental culture' or 'mental development'. Forms of meditation existed before the time of the Buddha, but his distinctive contribution was 'insight' meditation, which means careful observation of the feelings and thoughts that one has with the aim of seeing more clearly into the way things really are. 'Mental culture' has a wide meaning. It includes the more formal sitting and walking meditation, but it also includes awareness and mindfulness during all daily activities. Thus most born Buddhists do not constantly talk about meditation since they are aware of its complete meaning and it is a constant part of their daily life. It would be a mistake therefore to think that we do not practise mediation; it is rather that it is not the same type of meditation that would be practised on meditation retreats.

The Goonewardenes might join in a more formal guided meditation when visiting a monastery, but the children do not practise formal mediation:

> I can't sit crosslegged!

says Chula. Mrs Goonewardene does practice formal meditation, and also yoga for relaxation:

> I try to practise *mindfulness* in all situations, to concentrate on the present, when doing everyday things like washing-up. I also practise meditation on breathing and contemplation of the parts of the body. I find that it helps me feel revitalised and ready to go.

I asked the children who the Buddha is.

> He was the greatest man ever known in the whole world. He is special because he teaches you the right way of life. We don't know where he is now. Maybe we will all eventually join him somewhere. Eventually everyone will reach the state that the Buddha reached. It is something like all our thoughts put together.

What is the most important thing in Buddhism?

> The main theme running through Buddhism is to understand the Buddha's teaching and to live accordingly. The Buddha himself said that mere respect for the teacher is insufficient and that one has to live according to the Dhamma.

QUESTIONS

1 *Do you agree that everyone needs a code by which to live, and a religion and/or culture to which to belong?*

2 *Do you think it is important for children to know the language, religion and culture of their parents?*

3 *If you could give the world five moral precepts by which to live, what would they be?*

4 *Buddhist precepts are guidelines rather than inflexible rules. Can you see any advantages or disadvantages in this?*

5 *What do you think about the moral issues involved in going fishing, eating meat, finding money or drinking alcohol?*

6 *Do you know how many different religions are followed in your class, school, village or town?*

7 *Do you think it is a good idea to learn about religions in school, or should this be left to the Sunday or evening schools of each religion? As religious education is required by law, what do you think might be the most useful things to learn about. Should there be more or less religious education in the school curriculum?*

8 *Find out what the 1988 Education Reform Act lays down about religious education. In your opinion, should religious education be mostly Christian in this country?*

9 *Why do you think Buddhists have shrines and make offerings even though the Buddha is not a god and cannot answer prayers?*

10 *Do you think that we all need ceremonies at important times in our lives? Can you think of some ceremonies from other religions that mark important times in life? What about people with no religion?*

11 *Why do you think people go on pilgrimages even if this involves considerable travelling, money and hardship?*

12 *Why do lay Buddhists enjoy giving food to the monks?*

13 *If you could meet the Goonewardene family, what questions would you like to ask them?*

5

AYYA THANISSARA:
a woman's place in the meditative life
(Theravada)

Amaravati Daily Timetable

4 a.m.	Rising bell.
5 a.m.	Morning puja (chanting) and meditation.
7 – 8 a.m.	Morning meeting including breakfast and morning talk.
8 – 10.30 a.m.	Morning work. Alms round for monks and nuns.
10.30 a.m.	Meal offering.
12.30 p.m.	Tea break.
1 – 5 p.m.	Work.
5 p.m.	Tea break and informal chat.
7.30 – 9.30 p.m.	Evening puja and meditation followed by a talk from a senior member of the community.
10 or 11 p.m.	Bedtime (time decided by the individual).

I arrived at Amaravati, a large Buddhist vihara or monastery in the countryside near Hemel Hempstead, at about 2 p.m. having decided not to stop for lunch. I was in a hurry and on a diet anyway. I then found out that guests staying at the monastery were invited to keep to the monastery routine and to maintain the Eight Precepts for lay people observing a special religious occasion. I decided that it would be a good experience to observe the precepts for the time I spent at the monastery. This meant no food for me that day! I also took off my earrings. I was glad to find that 'no luxurious bed' meant a simple low bed rather than a mat on the ground.

The next morning I decided to observe the monastery routine, so I forced myself out of bed at 4 a.m. Morning puja involved the monks and nuns chanting sections of the Buddha's teaching in Pali and expressing their respect for the Buddha. The sound of the Pali chanting was very peaceful and calming – worth getting up for! The meditation which followed lasted about an hour and included breathing meditation, meditation on the body and meditation on love. If you are not used to it, it is easy for the body to become stiff with sitting in one position. I was relieved when 7 a.m. came and we could relax and have our porridge and tea (in the same cup, echoing the way that monks and nuns receive the food offered in one alms bowl, and saving washing-up!). I offered to join in with the work of the day and found myself sticking address labels on envelopes to send out the Amaravati newsletters. As the work was shared with a group of people it was quite enjoyable. Others did repairs or cooking or cleaning. I was quite pleased to see a monk rather than a nun doing the hoovering!

When I met Ayya Thanissara (*ayya* is the Pali word for a nun, meaning something like 'sister', and Thanissara means 'freedom of deliverance') my first questions were about the monastic routine. Is it hard having to get up at 4 a.m. every day?

> One of the Ten Precepts kept by nuns is 'to refrain from indulgence in sleep'. We have five to six hours of sleep a night, and sometimes may have half an hour's nap in the afternoon. It is not difficult because generally less sleep is needed when one meditates. Our lives are not hectic. If you feel sleepy, the meditative approach is to seek the causes of this sleepiness; you might be tired and need a rest or perhaps you are trying to escape a situation or avoid the difficulties that might arise during the course of the day.

Perhaps that is why I find it difficult to get up at any time of day! Once a week there is also an 'observance day', a day of silence when monks and nuns will stay awake all night in a vigil of meditation and chanting. On these days there is no morning puja or organised work.

Apart from the morning porridge, the monks and nuns have one meal a day, which must be over before midday. Monks and nuns cannot buy food or cook, so this meal is offered by lay people, who usually bring the food to the monastery. The monks and nuns are not allowed to ask for food and if no lay people make offerings the novices are allowed to prepare the meal.

> We will accept with gratitude whatever food is offered other than alcoholic drink. We prefer vegetarian food because we encourage non-violence and do not like animals to be killed for food. However, if meat was offered we would accept it, as the Buddha taught. If more food is placed in the bowl than you need, it may be given away – for example, sometimes I give left-over meat to the cats.

I was relieved to hear that monks and nuns did not have to eat absolutely everything placed in their bowls, a story that used to worry me as a child. What if something awful dropped into the bowl? As with sleep, if you get hungry you should use this as a basis for insight meditation on the feeling of hunger.

After midday we may sometimes have tea, fruit juice and a little of something sweet like boiled sweets, honey, sugar or dark chocolate. There are helpful if one has been working hard, and if we visit a lay person's home at teatime it is nice that there is something which they can offer.

The nuns of Amaravati do go on the traditional almsround with their bowls, although not every day. The nuns walk in silence in single file through nearby villages and towns. They do not look at people or ask for food. In Thailand people would be waiting to put food into their bowls, but this rarely happens in Britain. English people are usually too polite and may be embarrassed. People sometimes smile or ignore them; some people, even if not Buddhists, will say hello. The almsround is considered important even if no food is offered:

The image of a monk or nun on an almsround is an important symbol of the spiritual path, one of the Four Signs that Siddhartha saw which prompted his quest for enlightenment. It makes people think and wonder. It is good for the nun too, in that you have a contact with the society around you.

The nuns will stop and talk if someone talks to them, but generally they do not make the first move.

It is nice if people do speak and say hello.

The giving of food to monks and nuns, whether on almsround or in the monastery, is an important part of the close relationship between the monastic and lay communities. It is important for the lay people to have an opportunity to give, and for the monks and nuns to receive with gratitude. The lay people make the holy life possible. In return the monks and nuns give 'spiritual food' to the lay people by their teaching and example.

The nuns have shaved heads exactly like the monks but they wear brown robes. The nuns in Britain chose this colour themselves in order to distinguish themselves from the monks. Theravada monks generally wear bright yellow/orange robes, although the forest-dwelling monks wear a darker brownish-yellow colour.

The robes are a symbol both to ourselves and to others that we have adopted the path of renunciation. It is part of the simplification of life.

Sister Thanissara had given up pretty clothes, jewellery and cosmetics, but to my eyes she looked attractive in her brown robe even if a shaved head is unusual for a woman. For a few days afterwards I toyed with the idea of shaving my own head, but decided to keep the long hair to hide the growing wrinkles – exactly the sort of vanity and unwillingness to face reality that the life of renunciation is designed to uncover.

The monastic routine, the robes and shaved heads, the rites and customs are all means to an end. They turn the whole of life into meditation, and practising the conventions of the monastic life along with more formal meditation helps to develop a reflective mind:

> The heart of the monastic life is to be aware. This means understanding yourself, being sensitive to others, knowing how to work in the community and to fulfil your responsibilities. In this way you feel your place within the whole.
>
> Meditation is our life, learning to understand ourselves and the world around us, becoming more in touch with ourselves, our fears and desires, and those of the people around us. When we see how painful our fears and wrong desires are, we can let them go. In this way we come to know peace.

Formal meditation is practised in groups for two hours a day, and further meditation can be practised as individuals. Techniques include observing the breathing, observing the feelings in the body and observing the flow and change of the mind.

> The point of meditation is to be more aware and sensitive, open to the mystery of life. It helps to develop wisdom and compassion for others. We come to realise that we are all connected and that whatever we do or say or even think has an effect somewhere.

Theravada Buddhist nuns keep Ten Precepts, including the 'Five Precepts' for lay people (see p. 42), of which the most important is non-harming. As a nun, Ayya Thanissara lives a celibate life but, having given up the option to get married and have children, she finds that she sometimes spends time working with children who come to visit the monastery. The further five precepts are forms of renunication:

6 To refrain from eating after midday
7 To refrain from over-indulgence in sleep
8 To refrain from wearing ornaments
9 To refrain from going to shows or entertainment (including television)
10 To refrain from using silver, gold or money

Following these precepts helps to make you more open and less controlling. The precepts are very important as a foundation for developing the spiritual path. The whole basis of the Buddhist path is the observation of the first Five Precepts. These help us to do that which is good and refrain from that which causes harm to ourselves or others. In this way our minds become very clear and calm. From such a mind it is possible for wisdom and compassion to arise – the fruits of the spiritual path.

However, Buddhist morality is not a matter of following rules:

They are guidelines for training. If you make mistakes, that is something you can learn from rather than feel guilty about. They way of life outlined in the precepts springs naturally from living in a meditative way – you gradually find that you would not want to do anything that goes against the precepts. There are no fixed positions on right and wrong, you must judge every situation for yourself. This is a skill that needs wisdom and practice.

Thus on controversial moral issues,

There is no point in rushing in with a view for or against. Rather you should analyse the causes of something like violence and war, and examine the results of various courses of action.

Such a reflection can lead to taking positive action in your own life. Thinking about famine

Leads you to see how you can refrain from greed for the benefit of the whole. In the West, we need to simplify our lives so that we can share our resources with the poorer countries.

On the place of animals and care for the environment,

The planet is not just for humans. Reflection leads you to be grateful to animals for what they provide for us, to coexist with them rather than exploit them. We also respect plant life and accept our responsibility for the planet.

In the forest-dwelling tradition there is not much stress on studying scripture, but the most used section of the scripture is the Vinaya or rules for monastic discipline:

It is useful to know the rules and to see why the particular rules grew up, the stories surrounding them.

It is important to keep the spirit of the Vinaya, not only the letter of the law.

Some of it is now out of date. For example, at the time of the Buddha, nuns had always to travel in pairs as they were often attacked if by themselves. We still travel in pairs if we can, but may take safe public transport on our own. There are no rules covering modern inventions like television and cheques. Because of this some monks in Buddhist countries would think it acceptable to watch television and receive cheques, but we feel that this goes against the spirit of the rules about watching shows and receiving money.

A Buddhist monastery will contain a shrine room with an altar and a statue of the Buddha which is used for ceremonies like puja, meditation and the meal. There are separate meeting rooms for the monks and the nuns. There is simple sleeping accommodation for the monks and the nuns and for guests. The living accommodation is very simple. At Amaravati there is another hall for meetings and talks, and the Rainbow Room for children. Most monasteries will also have a *stupa*. A stupa is a dome-shaped monument based on the burial mounds or monuments placed over the relics of the Buddha. They usually contain a relic of some holy person and are sometimes painted white. The shapes involved are said by some Buddhists to symbolise the basic elements of the universe. The square base represents earth, the round dome represents water and the various conical shapes on top of the dome represent in turn fire, wind and space. The stupa reminds Buddhists of the Buddha and of the state of nirvana which lies beyond life as we know it. (The name of the monastery, Amaravati, meaning 'the deathless realm', also recalls this idea.) Stupas often include Buddha statues. The custom is to leave offerings like candles and flowers at a stupa and to walk clockwise around it three times as a sign of respect and as a way of remembering the Three Jewels: the Buddha, the Dharma and the Sangha. They also serve to remind people of the peace for which Buddhism aims, and several stupas have been built as symbols of peace between the peoples of the world.

When offerings are made to the Buddha statue, and the monks and nuns are chanting, it seems as if they are praying to a god, asking him to accept the offerings, forgive mistakes and so on. However, this may be a misleading impression:

Some people do like to think of the historical Buddha when they are performing their devotional ceremonies, but it is more important to realise that we are not communicating with an external being, but with the potential enlightenment within ourselves. 'Buddha' means to be awake and aware, so that anyone who is aware has a 'Buddha' mind. This means that they can see the Dhamma, the truth of life. The statues, offerings and prayers are simply techniques, symbols which help us.

Gautama the man died, but Buddha was never born and will never die. The Dhamma is both within you and outside of you; beyond time and place and all limitations. It is what is left when you let go of all limitations of personality, sex, nationality . . . the passing conditions. Buddha is not just in ancient history but present within us – wherever there is understanding, respect, compassion, wisdom and kindness. In this way the Buddha lives on.

Before she became a Buddhist nun, taking first ordination at the age of 23, Ayya Thanissara worked in Paris and attended art school. She was the daughter of Irish Catholics, but was interested in Eastern countries from an early age. At 19 she became interested in Buddhist meditation and went to live in a Buddhist community. At 22 she travelled to the East to study meditation further before being ordained.

Becoming a Buddhist is a gradual thing; you slowly find yourself following a Buddhist way of life.

However, because being a nun is a definite commitment,

First of all you become an *anagarika*, someone who has left behind their old life and who takes on eight of the Ten Precepts. This means that they can still handle money and go shopping, which makes them useful companions for the ordained. The emphasis is one service to the community and letting go of selfishness.

Anagarikas wear white robes. After two years an anagarika may go on to full ordination. The ceremony is a public event, and family and friends are invited. She must prove both to the community of monks and to the community of nuns that she is qualified to be ordained. A nun sews her own brown robe. She is given the Ten Precepts, and the bare necessities of the monastic life are donated – for example, her parents may supply a bowl. A nun receives a new name as a symbol of her new life.

Do nuns have the same status as monks?

The life of the nun is based on the same principles and way of life as that of the monk. In the general running of the monastery practical tasks are undertaken according to capability regardless of whether one is a monk or a nun; for example, both monks and nuns help out with cleaning the monastery and building work. All those who live in the monastery are given the same opportunities to develop spiritually. The

Buddha gave full ordination to women and made it clear that enlightenment is available to both sexes.

However, technically the nuns do not have the same status as the monks because the line of ordination for *bhikkhunis* (female monks) died out some centuries after the Budda. When bhikkhunis did exist, they took guidance from the monks

because the order of monks was established first and therefore they had more experience in living this lifestyle.

Thanissara explains that, in the culture of ancient India, women did not have so much freedom and were traditionally looked after by their father, husband or sons. The recorded words of the Buddha in the scriptures (Pali Canon) seem rather negative about women. He does not appear to have been very enthusiastic about admitting them to the ordained community. Some Buddhist women point out that the scriptures were written down by men and may not be the Buddha's exact words. In addition, the Buddha had to take into consideration the sort of society in which he lived; perhaps his attitude would be different today.

In countries like Thailand with a long Buddhist tradition, where full ordination is not possible, nuns may have to support themselves as quite often they do not receive as much support from society as the monks do. Besides developing their own spiritual life, they also like to help the monks by cooking their food. They wear the white of lay followers or novices rather than the robe. In Britain the nuns acknowledge the monks' seniority in small ways, for example by letting them pass first through a doorway and allowing them to be served first with the food offering. Would Thanissara like to re-establish full bhikkhuni ordination for women?

Whether we are technically fully ordained nuns or not is not important as we have evolved a way of life which works and can be lived according to the principles that the Buddha intended. Some feminists feel strongly that we should have full equality of status. Traditionalists feel strongly that because the line of ordination and training rules for nuns going back to the Buddha have been lost it is impossible for anyone to reinstitute it. Ordination is only valid if it can be traced back in a line of teachers to the Buddha himself. I don't think that it is worth upsetting people over. Besides, the bhikkhuni rules we read in the scriptures were very strict and it would probably be very difficult to observe all the rules in this society. I think we have more ability to adapt to this present society with our current arrangements!

What attracted Thanissara towards this way of life?

From an early age Buddhist teachings made sense to me. I first heard of *rebirth* when I was about 12; it seemed to make a lot of sense to me. After all, meditation shows us that the mind constantly changes from one state to another.

Rebirth cannot be proved or disproved:

It is not something that you can argue about rationally, more of an insight into the nature of mind that comes from meditation.

What appeals to me most about Buddhism is that it is a teaching based on transcending the limitations that as human beings we live with. It helps you become more in touch with yourself, with the inner source of your life. You come to realise that our true nature is the unifying force that we are all part of, rather than the limited personality we tend to identify as 'ourself'. Our true nature is a mind unlimited, clear, compassionate and wise. The conventions of Buddhism are a clear practical way to this realisation.

QUESTIONS

1 *Do you think you could adapt to the monastic routine? What aspects of it would you like or dislike? What is the point of having the day structured in this way?*

2 *Have you ever met a Buddhist monk or nun? If so, how did you feel when meeting them? If not, how do you think you would have reacted before you studied Buddhism? Would you react differently now?*

3 *In the Zen monastery the monks and nuns did watch television. What are the arguments for and against monks and nuns watching television?*

4 *Make a list of all the things that most girls and women enjoy that Theravada nuns renounce. Which of these would you miss most? Why do nuns renounce all these things?*

5 *How does formal practice of meditation (at least two hours a day) affect the daily life of a nun?*

6 *Why are the moral precepts described as guidelines rather than fixed rules? What are the advantages and disadvantages of this?*

7 *Why do Buddhists like to build stupas and shrines? Why do people like to visit them? What do they do when they visit a shrine and a stupa?*

8 *Does equality for women mean that women do exactly the same things as men?*

9 *Do you think Theravada Buddhist nuns have 'equality of opportunity' with Buddhist monks?*

10 *What is an anagarika in the British Theravada tradition? Can you think of occasions when an anagarika could provide a useful service to the sangha or community of monks and nuns?*

11 *Discuss arguments for and against the Buddhist teaching that we live many lives rather than just one. Can this question be decided by arguments, or is it a matter of feelings?*

12 *What practical differences do you think it would make to the way you behaved, if you thought of yourself as part of a unifying force in the universe, rather than as a separate individual 'self'?*

13 *If you could talk to Ayya Thanissara, what other questions would you ask her?*

6

MIKE HOOKHAM:
Vajrayana, the power of communication
(Nying ma pa)

Mike Hookham is a married lay teacher in the Nying ma pa tradition of Tibetan Buddhism. His house in Oxford is the headquarters of the Longchen Foundation and the Nitartha School for the teaching of Nying ma Buddhism. At present he has between 30 and 40 students who come regularly to meetings at his house, or in London. It is almost a full-time job, but in order to make ends meet Mike also undertakes some tutoring in maths and computing.

Mike's house is full of books – not all on Buddhism – which have overflowed to fill a cabin in the garden. We talked about how precious books are in the Tibetan tradition. Scriptural texts are always carefully wrapped in cloth and placed above other objects in the room for

> Texts represent the speech of Buddahood.

In fact to Tibetans not just scriptures but all books are very precious and are treated with great care, for

> Language itself, the power of communication, is sacred.

I mentioned to Mike that one Tibetan Buddhist who visited my house criticised the fact that my 'Dharma books' (books on Buddhism) were mixed up on my bookshelves with other books. Was that a common attitude?

> In the modern Western world respect for books is not the same because we have so many. Even respecting 'Dharma books' can be difficult when you have a lot. You should respect books as far as is practical. Tibetan lamas have been known to pile books on the floor when studying.

I was relieved to find that my bookshelves would not offend all Tibetan Buddhists.

When I arrived at Mike's house he was busy at his computer – not the usual picture of a Buddhist teacher. Mike studied maths and physics at university, and has worked in the atomic energy industry and with computers. He sees no contradiction between modern science and technology and the ancient traditions of Buddhism. Both physics and Buddhism explore the nature of the universe and are based on direct experience. However, as a teenager Mike decided that Buddhism was like science but better because it was not limited to the intellectual but also involved the direct experience of meditation and one's mind and emotions.

Mike's involvement with Buddhism has been a long one. His first contact with it was back in 1944 as a nine-year-old schoolboy. One of the books he read at school was about a Thai village and included a chapter where a monk was telling the story of the Buddha to the village children. The story of the prince who gave up all his luxury in order to search for something that would benefit others made a deep impression. Later, as a sixth-former, Mike started to read about different religions and came across the well-known paperback by Christmas Humphreys, the late president of the Buddhist Society. Although decades later Mike can see deficiencies in the book, at the time it served to introduce Mike, and many others, to a lifetime involvement with Buddhism:

> I was tremendously impressed that you could have such a different view of the universe from the basically Christian one with which I had been brought up. Such vastness of time and space, such emphasis on direct experience through meditation.

By the age of 21, Mike had decided that he actually was a Buddhist and needed to do more than just read about it in books. He started to attend classes at the London Buddhist Society where he learned about Theravada, Tibetan and Zen Buddhism. At that time, in 1956, the Theravada tradition was the only one properly established and Mike studied Theravada meditation with bhikkhus who had trained and had been ordained in Thailand. However, meditation proved to be not as easy as it seemed, and he was attracted to the Mahayana teachings brought by Sangharakshita in 1962:

> I realised the need for the emotional side of faith and devotion. Buddhahood is something beyond yourself that you are not going to attain by your own efforts.

Up until then Mike had been rather critical of religion based on faith and devotion, looking for help outside of oneself, but he found that the practices he had dismissed as an unthinking sort of religion were actually helpful if taken in the right way.

Sangharakshita left to form his own Buddhist organisation, the

Western Buddhist Order. Meanwhile Mike met Chogyam Trungpa Rinpoche, an important Tibetan lama who had fled from the Chinese invasion of 1959, and he realised that he had found his teacher. He spent whole weekends in Oxford with Chogyam Trungpa, going through texts and talking about Tibetan Buddhism:

> These were the most important days of my life.

In Tibetan Buddhism your teacher (guru or lama) is very important. Although books are precious, Buddhism cannot be learned from them alone; one must have a personal transmission of the teachings from someone who has himself received the transmission:

> In a sense to you he is the Buddha, transmitting the teaching. He is like a kind parent, giving you the best thing that he has.

It is important to find the teacher who is right for you, perhaps spending a few years with them first. Sometimes people know instantly that they have found the right person. Another Tibetan Buddhist told me that when first meeting her lama, 'The whole physical atmosphere changed when he was present.'

Chogyam Trungpa was a teacher in the Kargyu pa tradition of Buddhism. Like many famous Tibetan lamas, he was said to be a *tulku* – the reincarnation of a particular holy man of the past who had decided to return to the world in order to help others. When a tulku dies, a search is made for a baby who is his reincarnation. While visiting one Tibetan Buddhist group I was introduced to a smiling baby who had been identified as the reincarnation of their recently deceased teacher. There are several ways of identifying such babies; they may recognise their old friends and possessions, or a lama may have a vision or dream about the place where they are to be found.

Mike took Chogyam Trungpa as his teacher in 1965. There were three stages in this process, corresponding to the three 'yanas' or 'vehicles' of Buddhism. Tibetan Buddhism claims to embrace all the traditions of Buddhism, and the massive collections of scriptures and commentaries (the Kanjur and Tenjur) contain scriptures from Hinayana, Mahayana and Vajrayana Buddhism.

The first ceremony was to 'take refuge', which in Tibetan Buddhism means taking refuge in, expressing your commitment to and looking for guidance from, the Buddha, Dharma and the Sangha, and also in the lama. You make offerings of flowers, incense and light on the shrine, and the lama cuts off a piece of your hair. You repeat the formula of taking refuge three times and receive a new name. This is the Hinayana stage, where your main concern is your own spiritual development.

A year after 'taking refuge' Mike was introduced to the Mahayana by taking the bodhisattva vow. At this stage you are thinking of others rather than yourself:

> You must at least aspire to the attitude of abandoning your welfare to the welfare of others.

Again you make offerings and a solemn vow, dedicating youself to working towards enlightenment in order that you may help others towards enlightenment: 'Just like the earth . . . may I become a source of nourishment . . . for all beings situated throughout space until they reach the highest peace.' This is a very serious step and cannot be taken lightly. Your teacher may require you to wait. From this point on you are

> a member of the Buddha's family; an immature buddha rather than totally different.

A bodhisattva is a being who, as in this ceremony, has vowed to achieve enlightenment but not to pass into nirvana until all beings are saved. The word may be used to refer to a human being like Mike who has taken this vow, or to

> beings higher than ourselves up to just before Buddhahood.

Advanced bodhisattvas can appear in many forms. They may take human form, as in the case of a tulku, or they may appear in a 'heavenly' form such as people have experienced in meditation. It is the advanced bodhisattvas who are represented in images on Mahayana shrines. For example, Mike's shrine has a stature of *Avalokitesvara* or *Chenrezi* with many arms, symbolising his compassionate help for all beings. All of the bodhisattvas and buddhas, except the eternal Buddha, were once human beings, but they are now able to help those who pray to them. They also embody the different aspects of Buddhahood – compassion, wisdom, etc. – and so are not like gods to be worshipped as completely separate from oneself; rather, they stand for what one is trying to develop within oneself.

The third stage of Mike's development in Tibetan Buddhism was the Vajrayana. It is considered to be a faster but more dangerous path to enlightenment, which is why guidance from a personal teacher is particularly important. It is dangerous because it involves working with the emotions, even the negative ones like hatred and anger.

For each particular aspect of Vajrayana you go through a ceremony called 'abhisheka', or 'empowerment'. You are told the history of the practice, and make the usual offerings. Water is poured on your head and given you to drink, symbolising purification and concecration. Each ceremony usually centres on one particular 'yidam' or 'deity', such as a particular bodhisattva. During the ceremony you think of the teacher as taking on the form of the deity, and that this yidam is passed from the teacher to yourself:

> If this doesn't happen in actuality, then the whole thing is merely a ceremony, not a real empowerment.

The teacher will read you the particular text, explain its meaning and how to do the practice, and then you may receive the scripture itself. The transmission of the text in this way is known as the '*lung*' and the explanation as 'ti'. Without this transmission from the teacher, reading the text by itself can be very misleading and confusing. Other Tibetan Buddhists have expressed concern to me that Vajrayana texts are nowadays easily available in printed book form, which can lead to considerable misunderstanding.

The Buddhist teachings that Mike finds most significant are the related doctrines of 'no self', 'emptiness' and 'the interpenetration of all things'. This sounded rather difficult, so I asked Mike to explain.

> The anatta or 'no self' teaching focuses on our emotional feelings about things. The tendency is to feel that 'my car' is a single thing; you don't think of it as a lot of parts. Intellectually you know that it is made up of parts, but emotionally you behave to things as if they were separate solid entities. The language we use to label things suggests that things are single, solid and unchanging whereas they are really composite and changing.

This applies to people as well as cars.

The Mahayana teaching of 'emptiness' goes somewhat further:

> Not only are things made up of parts, but even the parts are not solid, separate or unchanging. Physics says much the same thing. Our usual emotional attitude is to solidify, separate and label things: for example, one speaks of a person as one thing although really body, mind and speech are a continuing process that cannot be pinned down by a label.

So 'emptiness' does not mean 'nothingness', that nothing really exists, rather that things do not exist in a solid, separate and unchanging form but are dynamically linked together in a never-ending process. Why use the rather negative term 'emptiness'?

> Well, it is very hard to put it positively without giving the wrong impression. Really it cannot be put into words or understood with the mind. It can only be understood by Buddha vision.

One of Mike's favourite scriptures is the Heart Sutra which centres on the teaching of 'emptiness'.

The 'interpenetration of all things' is a similar but more positively expressed teaching found in the Avatamsaka sutra. Everything that exists is interconnected and interdependent:

> This does not just apply to things in the world but to enlightenment itself. The Buddha essence is in everything that exists. Buddhahood is the nature of all things but we do not see things as they really are.

The purpose of the practices of Buddhism, ceremony and meditation is to

> learn to open oneself out and experience this real nature of things.

Tibetan Buddhism contains many different ways of doing this. If the Buddha nature is in all things you could really attempt to experience Buddhahood by

> surrendering to a piece of dirt in the road.

However, in practice it is very difficult to see the Buddha in a piece of dirt and much more effective to attempt to see the Buddha in a living teacher or an image of a Buddha or bodhisattva. This explains the great reverence shown to lamas and to the images of the shrine, and why in Tibetan Buddhism we refer to the Buddha nature as existing only in living beings.

Respect for images, scriptures and teachers is very important in Tibetan Buddhism. Texts and images are placed on a high shelf or altar and the lama will sit on a higher seat than the pupil. The seat is often beautifully covered in bright brocades. Ways of showing respect to images include holding it on top of your head, never picking the statue up by its head, never pointing at it with your finger or feet, and never breathing on it. Candles and incense offered on the shrine should not be blown out but allowed to burn down naturally or snuffed out. A distinction is made between images that are empty and unblessed and those which have been 'consecrated' by a teacher. This means that the teacher will have placed a relic and perhaps a piece of scripture inside the statue and might have passed on a meditation practice connected with that particular image

so that it becomes a channel to lead you towards realisation.

Although such images are treated with great reverence, it is not really the object but 'your own openness' that leads to insight, as is shown by the following traditional story:

A Tibetan trader was going on an expedition to India, where the Buddha's teaching originated. His mother asked him to bring her back a precious relic of the Buddha and he promised that he would. He went off on his travels and had lots of adventures, visited Buddhist shrines and monasteries and successfully sold all his stock of goods. He was almost back at his home village when suddenly remembered his old mother's request. Seeing a dog's skeleton by the roadside, he decided to take one of the dog's teeth and give it to the old lady. 'I'll say that it is a tooth of the Buddha, all the way from India. She'll never know the difference,' he thought. The old lady received the tooth with grateful thanks. She placed it on her shrine and made offerings of flowers and incense with great faith and devotion. As time went by, everyone in the village was amazed to see a halo of golden light appearing around the tooth.

Mike commented that

The dog's tooth became a relic because of the faith that the old lady had. It was not just the belief she had about the tooth as such but using her faith and devotion as a basis for meditation, enabling her to see clearly and give up her false view of the world. The tooth became a channel for enlightenment to come into the world.

Mike's own shrine contains many images. There is a large golden statue of Buddha Shakyamuni, of other buddhas and bodhisattvas, and pictures of teachers living and dead. One of the images is of *Padmasambhava*, the enlightened teacher who introduced Buddhism to Tibet in the eighth century. He is looked upon as the founder of the Nying ma pa tradition. Although Mike's teacher, who died in 1987, was of the Kargyu pa tradition, he also taught Nying ma and considered that it would be a useful tradition to establish in Britain as it stresses lay people rather than monks. Lamas are often married in this tradition. Padmasambhava is also called *Guru Rinpoche* or 'precious teacher' and Mike is hoping to establish a pilgrimage centre dedicated to Guru Rinpoche in North Wales.

On a separate table I noticed two objects called the *vajra* (diamond-thunderbold-sceptre) and bell. These objects are held in the right and left hands during certain Vajrayana ceremonies and symbolise the two sides of enlightenment or Buddhahood. The bell represents wisdom and the vajra compassion. The bell is thought of as feminine and the vajra as masculine: both are needed for completeness.

I asked about meditation practices and ceremonies.

> Our basic practice is called 'formless meditation', which is basically sitting crosslegged and meditating on the outbreath, following the mind and experiences that arise without judging. Yes, it is rather like zazen.

As you progress, more advanced practices are added, corresponding to the bodhisattva vow and the various Vajrayana consecrations. One common practice is called the 'sevenfold puja', which comes from a Mahayana scripture. The seven stages are:

1 Paying homage to Buddhahood, perhaps represented for you by one particular buddha or bodhisattva figure.
2 Making offerings: food, flowers, candles, incense, etc.
3 Confessing or admitting your faults.
4 Rejoicing in the good done by others, buddhas and ordinary people too.
5 Requesting the buddhas to teach.
6 Requesting the buddhas and bodhisattvas not to pass away into nirvana but to stay and help others.
7 Dedicating the merit of the ceremony to all beings.

This puja can be performed physically, with real offerings and prostrations before an actual image, or it can be performed mentally.

Those who practise Vajrayana may celebrate a 'ganachakra' ceremony on the tenth and twenty-fifth days of the lunar month. This involves a feast of food, all of which is prepared as nicely as possible and must include meat and alcohol. 'Another practice is the 'fire puja', whereby things like flour, grain, milk, water and alcohol are offered in a fire outside. This ceremony is performed at the beginning or end of a new project. As the smoke rises into the atmosphere and spreads out, so do the offerings one is making. Amongst other things, this is a ceremony connected with protecting the environment. Tibetans have traditionally been very concerned about the environment and for that reason do not like interfering with nature. They do not even like mining the earth, which to them is a living thing. 'Guru yoga' is a Vajrayana practice in which you visualise (see in the mind) the form of a particular teacher of the past, realising that he is the same as your own teacher, and make offerings.

Typical of Vajrayana is an elaborate use of ceremonial and symbol. As well as those already mentioned there are the reciting of mantras, short prayers or sacred syllables connected to a particular buddha or bodhisattva, like 'om mani padme hum' for Avalokitesvara, called Chenrezi in Tibetan; the forming of mudras or symbolic gestures with the hands; and the constructing of mandalas or patterns based on the circle with coloured sands or paint. Tibetans also use prayer beads, prayer wheels and prayer flags so that emblems of their religion are to be seen everywhere.

I was surprised to hear about the eating of meat and the drinking of alcohol as part of a Buddhist ceremony. In Tibet the eating of meat and the drinking of alcohol, especially beer, are common and not frowned upon, although overindulgence is discouraged and vegetarians are much admired. When 'taking refuge', you can make a selection from the Five Precepts rather than taking all of them:

> For instance, you may take three of the Five Precepts, those against killing, stealing and lying, but leave out 'celibacy' and 'no alcohol'.

In any case, some Vajrayana practices deliberately involve the use of things like alcohol and meat that others consider forbidden.

Nying ma pa Buddhists are guided in moral behaviour by the Five Precepts and the Ten Virtuous Actions of Buddhist tradition: avoiding killing, stealing, sexual misconduct, false speech, harsh speech, malicious speech, idle speech, covetousness, ill-will and false views. However, as Mike mentioned, individuals may choose to opt out of one or more of the Five Precepts, and any of them may be overridden if the situation seems to demand it. When taking the bodhisattva vow, one takes 64 other precepts. These include not praising yourself and disparaging others, never refusing a gift because it might discourage generosity in others, not destroying the environment, helping the sick, never criticising other forms of religious truth except for the purpose of discussion, never criticising the words of a teaching rather than trying to understand its message, stopping others doing evil even if this means using force, never disparaging women (technically a Vajrayana precept) and fitting in with others. One common habit to which the Nying ma pa tradition is opposed is smoking:

> It makes you ill and can affect unborn children. It makes children irritable and uncontrolled and makes the mind dull.

Buddhists have a rather different approach to death and dying from the majority of other people:

> It is important to be aware when dying; drugs may be taken to subdue pain, but are not a good idea if they make the mind cloudy. Life should not be extended artificially.

It is at times of great suffering like death that Buddhism really makes sense. Mike himself has had cancer of the colon and suffered the death of his mother and of a girlfriend who also had cancer.

> Having practised meditation you have something ready when these traumatic events occur. You see the truth of the Buddha's teaching about suffering and impermanence, and how to cope by extending your sense of suffering from your own suffering to that of others. It's not that the suffering goes away – it becomes more in a sense – but you see it in a much vaster context. You realise that everybody feels like this. Instead of thinking 'why should it happen to me?', you think 'why shouldn't it happen to me?'. You see yourself as an example of everybody else rather than being tied up with just yourself, and somehow that becomes a great inspiration.

In Tibetan Buddhist belief there is an intermediate state between death and rebirth known as the 'bardo'. This is said to last 49 days, during which time the person passes through various experiences described in a scripture known as the Tibetan Book of the Dead. The experiences include the light of enlightenment, visions of buddhas and bodhisattvas, an illusion of being judged on your good and bad actions, and seeing your future parents. It is possible to achieve enlightenment during this time if you understand what is happening. Thus the text is read to the dying and the dead.

> Some teachers say that the real effect is on the living people hearing the text. The scripture affects your mind and as you are close to the dead person they could actually connect with the inspiration in your mind. Other people feel that it is really too late to help the dead person as they have already gone according to their karma, and so the emphasis is on practising here and now, before you die.

Although Tibetan Buddhism has a complex collection of scriptures, images, ceremonies and symbols, it is clear that it is all geared to the traditional goals of Buddhism: to understand suffering, the cause of it and how to be liberated from it, to reach enlightenment and see reality as it really is, and to work compassionately for all beings.

QUESTIONS

1 *Nying ma pa lamas are often married, unlike monks in other traditions of Buddhism. What do you think are the advantages and disadvantages of a religious teacher or minister being married?*

2 *In what ways are sacred books treated with respect in other religions?*

3 *Why do Tibetan Buddhists 'take refuge' in the lama as well as the Buddha, the Dharma and the Sangha? Why is such respect shown to lamas?*

4 *The transmission of texts, especially Vajrayana ones, is surrounded by ceremony. In order to practise the meditation described in the text, you need the 'lung' and 'ti' of the teacher. However, nowadays the same texts can be bought by anyone from a bookshop. How far do you think that sacred texts should be available to anyone to read in their own language? Can you see the advantages and disadvantages of this? What happens in other religions at present and in the past?*

5 *Why does Tibetan Buddhism have such a vast collection of scriptures, images, symbols and ceremonies?*

7

YÖNTEN GYATSO:
a happy mind (Ge lug pa)

According to Yönten Gyatso, Buddhism is all about happiness:

> The most precious thing that Buddhism offered me was keeping a happy mind. I don't mean a selfish sort of happiness. Selfishness always leads to unhappiness. Happiness depends on your own mind, not external conditions. Practising Buddhism, going through each day putting others first, you get happier and happier. You have a whale of a time, it's good fun!

Like other Buddhist monks to whom I have spoken, Yönten Gyatso did seem to be a happy, contented person. He smiled and laughed a lot, and spoke with a quiet, gentle but confident tone.

He lives at the Madhyamaka Centre at Kilnwick Percy, 15 miles from York, which has been set up as a Buddhist community and centre for teaching. How do the locals react to the robe and the presence of Buddhists?

> It is a small rural community so we must seem strange, but everyone has been very friendly.

Yönten Gyatso – whose family still call him Mark – is 23, and has been a Buddhist for about two and a half years and a trainee monk for almost two of those. He admits to jumping in at the deep end. He originates from Manchester and still has the accent; he has studied at art college and worked as an electrician. I was interested to know why someone of his age, too young to have been around when Eastern religions and the 'hippy trail' to India were fashionable, was attracted towards Buddhism:

> I was looking for a more wholesome sort of life and knew that I had to start working on my uncontrolled mind. I was looking for some sort of teachings or guidance.

He attributes finding Buddhism to good fortune as he just happened to move to York and meet Buddhists from the centre. However, in Buddhist thought nothing happens by chance but rather by the law of cause and effect, karma. The actions of your earlier life or lives bring you to certain situations. Yönten Gyatso claims that the real cause of him finding Buddhism was the kindness of the guru, which in one sense refers to a particular human guru, and in a deeper sense to the infinite kindness of the Buddha.

Tibetan Buddhism lays particular emphasis on finding a guru or teacher (in Tibetan, lama):

> A guru is a holy enlightened being who has taken a rebirth in human form to help other people.

The guru whom Yönten found so impressive was a Tibetan lama called Geshe Kelsang Gyatso. Is Geshe Kelsang Gyatso actually enlightened, a buddha?

> That's not important: even if he is ordinary we have faith that he is Buddha and can seek Buddha's inspiration and help through him.

Yönten spoke at length about the importance of faith:

> The essence of real spiritual progress is faith, not so much in a particular man but in enlightened being.

Faith in the Buddha, the Dharma and the Sangha is expressed by taking the Three Refuges, which Yönten first took in the presence of his guru with 40 other people in a simple ceremony. Yönten told a Tibetan story to illustrate the importance of faith in religious practice:

> There was once a great famine in Tibet. The mother of a monk was starving, and her lama told her to recite a special mantra and stone would turn into bread. The woman's faith was so great that this happened. When her son the monk came to visit, he heard the story and told his mother that she had been saying the mantra all wrong. Her faith was lost and the miracle no longer happened.

Many people, especially in today's world, have problems with faith – for example, believing that story! However, you can start to practise Buddhism without much faith; there are other starting points such as anxiety about death, or an interest in meditation.

How do you know which teacher or set of teachings to have faith in? In Tibetan Buddhism the teachers can point to an unbroken lineage of pupils and teachers that goes back to the Buddha. Teachers should also be holy people who set a good example. You know teachings are valid if they actually help you in practice; as the Buddha himself said, whatever doctrines lead to dispassion, detachment, decrease of cravings, contentment, energy and delight in good are true doctrines. In the end it is something very personal, as with the deep impression made on Yönten by lama Kelsang Gyatso, who seemed to have special inner qualities. This is explained by Buddhists as being due to the law of karma:

> Different lamas have different connections with different people.

An inner certitude comes when you find your particular teacher.

Yönten was ordained in 1987. He is a *genyen*, which means that he took eight vows. The next stage is the *getsu* or novice monk who takes 33 vows, and then the fully fledged monk or *gelong* with over 200 vows to keep. The Ge lug pa tradition stresses the need to take things gradually, to do what is within your capabilities, to stay happy. Rushing ahead can lead to disappointment and loss of faith. Yönten does, however, consider himself to be a monk and at his ordination ceremony he had his head shaved and received the robe. The Tibetan robe is rather different from that of a Theravada monk. The colour is mainly burgundy with yellow for the outer robe:

> The darker colour suited the colder climate of Tibet.

The robe identifies you to others as a monk, and reminds you of the vows that you must keep so as to give a good example. Details of the robe are symbolic, such as the four folds in the 'skirt' to remind you of the Four Noble Truths.

Can women be ordained?

> Nuns have the same status as monks and wear similar robes. The bodhisattva *Tara* is said to have deliberately taken rebirth every time as a female to show that it doesn't matter what sex you are.

However, technically, as in the Theravada tradition, the nuns do not have the same status as monks because the line of ordination has died out.

Yönten's day starts at 6.30 a.m. After a wash and a cup of tea he will spend about an hour before his own personal shrine in puja and meditation. All the monks have a small shrine in their own room at the centre. Yönten's shrine has a statue of Buddha Shakyamuni, a small stupa, a text of scripture, a picture of his guru, a picture of Tara and seven offering bowls.

> I make three full-length prostrations, and an offering of water and incense. This takes about five minutes, and then I will meditate.

Meditation should be something to look forward to, so it must not go on too long. Then there is breakfast followed by work. Daily work might include painting, preparing for courses or making food. One of Yönten's daily tasks is to tidy up the *gompa* or shrine room, hoovering, arranging the cushions and making all the offerings on the shrine:

> By dedicating your actions for the welfare of all beings, and imagining all the buddhas happy with your offerings, it can be fun.

At 10 a.m. the community comes together for puja and meditation lasting for about 45 minutes. This involves chanting special services from set texts, in English on weekdays and in Tibetan on special occasions. Following the puja there are further prayers in the second, smaller shrine room.

Lunch is a noisy social occasion and the food served is vegetarian. The afternoon brings more work, study and meditation. Monks will not normally eat again, unless they are doing hard physical work in which case they have a small snack later in the day. Sometimes a particular ceremony may involve sharing food that has been offered on the shrine. From 7 p.m. until 8.30 there is teaching from one of the senior monks, usually open to everyone. Yönten's final tasks are to clean the kitchen and take all the offerings down from the shrine. He will then have tea and go to bed at about 11 p.m. or 12 midnight.

There are special days and festivals. Every full-moon day is dedicated to Tara. Tara is a female bodhisattva who is full of compassion and help for beings. She is said once to have been a princess and she brings a motherly and feminine element into Buddhism. Also once a month there is a special puja for the 'medicine Buddha', Bhaishajaguru. This buddha is said to be especially concerned with sickness and suffering. The puja prays for relief of sickness and suffering in the world. At the time of my visit the community were particularly concerned with a local farmer who enjoys shooting and whom the community feels is cruel to animals.

I arrived some days after a special ceremony had been performed by a visiting lama for the 'long life' of those taking part. I had previously read in books on Tibet that small pellets of food were eaten in a ceremony for long life. I was pleased to be offered one of these 'long-life pills', particularly when they turned out to be made of marzipan! I later found out that the real focus of the ceremony was not long life for the people involved in the ceremony, but 'long Life' for the buddhas and bodhisattvas, asking them to remain in the world to help beings rather than pass away into nirvana.

Annual festivals follow the Tibetan calendar. Tibetan New Year is in February, as is Chinese New Year. The first 15 days of the year commemorate the Buddha's early life. People visit shrines and make offerings. Traditionally this is the time for monks to take examinations for higher degrees which are conducted in great public debates.

In May the Buddha's enlightenment and death are celebrated. This may coincide with the Theravada Wesak but this is not necessarily the case as the calendars are different. Tibetans will take the Eight Precepts, which means fasting after midday and giving up eating meat. In July the Buddha's first teaching is celebrated, on Dharmachakra Day. Again this is near to but not the same as the day of the Theravada celebration. In Tibet, scriptures are carried in processions and people enjoy themselves by having picnics in the summer weather.

On 31 October the 'descent from the Tushita heavens' is celebrated. This recalls a story in the scriptures when the Buddha returned from preaching to his deceased mother in a heaven world. This occurs at roughly the same time as the Chinese festival of 'hungry ghosts' and the Theravada festival at the end of the monks' retreat season, which in Burma is also associated with the story of the Buddha's preaching to his mother.

One festival special to the Ge lug pa tradition is the celebration of the anniversary of Je Tsong Kha Pa, the founder of the tradition. Je Tsong Ka Pa was a fifteenth-century Tibetan monk who insisted on strict discipline in the monasteries which followed his tradition. Unlike in the Nying ma pa tradition, unmarried monks were emphasised rather than married teachers. Monks were to remain celibate and not to drink alcohol. The Ge lug pa tradition grew to be the most powerful in Tibet, and it is from this tradition that the spiritual and political ruler of Tibet was drawn from the seventeenth century until 1959. This famous 'Dalai Lama' is a tulku, and the current Dalai Lama is considered to be the fourteenth reincarnation of a fifteenth-century holy man who was the nephew and disciple of Je Tsong Kha Pa. The Dalai Lama is also thought to be an embodiment of the power of Chenrezi, the bodhisattva of compassion. The Chinese takeover of Tibet means that the Dalai Lama at present lives in exile in India.

The importance of festivals, according to Yönten, is that

> On some special days the karma or effects of your good and bad actions are multiplied a thousandfold. So you must be particularly mindful on those days and be sure to do good.

The community also celebrates birthdays and even Christmas!

The main shrine or gompa is in a large room that used to be a ballroom. The shrine itself takes up a whole wall and is crowded with statues, pictures, flowers and offerings. All the Tibetan shrines I have seen have been much more elaborate than other Buddhist shrines and very brightly coloured. The largest central figure is of Buddha Shakyamuni, a golden statue. The other statues are of buddhas, bodhisattvas and lamas. Among the images on the shrine were Chenrezi (called Avalokitesvara in India and Kwannon in Japan), Tara the saviouress, and Manjusri the bodhisattva of wisdom, who is represented holding a book and a sword. Some of the images on the shrine are in the form of golden statues, others are framed pictures and others still are in the traditional *thangka* form. A thangka is an image painted on cloth, usually with ornate brocade borders.

On the shrine there are several rows of offering bowls. In Tibetan practice there should be seven bowls and the offerings should include everything you would offer to a guest. The bowls contain water for drinking, water for washing, perfumed water, flowers, incense, candles and food. There may also be a small instrument to represent welcoming music. The food and drink offered looked very tempting – chocolate cakes and tropical fruit juice!

A particular feature of Tibetan Buddhism is the offering of *termas*, elaborately decorated yellow and red food sculptures. In Tibet these are traditionally made of butter, but in England where butter would melt the termas are made of marzipan. Several of the pictures and statues were draped with *katas*, white silk scarves that are traditional signs of respect in Tibet. There were many vases filled with colourful flowers, both fresh and dried. Yönten had certainly done his best to make the shrine beautiful.

On the left of the main shrine is a side altar to Vajrayogini, a female figure associated with Vajrayana practices. In the Ge lug pa tradition Vajrayana is not for beginners, who should concentrate on more basic practices. In front of the shrine is a raised seat or throne, covered with rich, colourful fabrics. This is for the lamas when they are teaching and is a way of showing respect.

Could Yönten Gyatso help us to make sense of the vast collection of buddhas, bodhisattvas and other holy figures in Tibetan Buddhism?

> They are all really Buddha. They are a big show put on by the buddhas to attract and increase faith. They are not separate beings. They are a help, a refuge, an inspiration.

When asked to explain further, Yönten talked of the *Trikaya* doctrine, the teaching that there are three forms of Buddha:

> What Buddha means is anyone who has removed all faults and perfected all good qualities. This means a mind that has perfect compassion, perfect power, perfect wisdom and cherishes each being as his only child. It implies omniscience, not in the sense of knowing all the details of the latest design in cars or whatever, but knowing the wish of every being, what is going to happen to them and how to help them. What Buddha is then is pure mind. This is beyond our imagination.

This 'pure mind' is the true form of the Buddha(s). For the sake of all unenlightened beings who cannot imagine pure mind, Buddha can appear or manifest in two other forms. There is the 'glorious body', when beautiful coloured forms appear as if made of light. These are the various bodhisattvas and buddhas that people have seen in visions and that the colourful pictures of Chenrezi, Tara and so on try to capture. It is easier for people to relate to a human-shaped figure than to the more abstract pure mind. The third form is the 'emanation body', which means that buddhas can take rebirth in earthly form in order to help others, the most famous example being Shakyamuni. The tulkus in Tibetan Buddhism are also examples of the emanation body. The important thing to remember is that

> All the 'deities' are manifestations of the one mind.

As all beings are potential buddhas,

> In a sense becoming Buddha means mixing up with that mind, that reality. You no longer have a strong sense of separate individuality, you have to leave your old self behind.

This is very difficult to explain, according to Yönten, because only when you become Buddha can you know what Buddha is. Meanwhile we should not worry too much about all this and should get on with Buddhist practice.

Buddhist practice for Yönten involves meditation and puja, living a moral life and studying Buddhism. 'Meditation, morality and wisdom' is a phrase often used to sum up the Buddhist way of life.

> Buddha taught many different meditations. The point of them all is to familiarise the mind with wholesome mind. This helps eradicate our self-grasping mind and has a direct result in our everyday life.

Helpful meditations include meditating on love, compassion, the impermanence of all things, the inevitability of death and the preciousness of human life:

> Meditation on the precious human life means you think how lucky you are to have been born a human who can practise Buddha's teachings. So many beings are insects, animals; so many humans are too hungry, miserable or handicapped to practise Buddhism, or have never heard of it.

This meditation and the meditation on death lead you to make the most of life while you can. There is also meditation on 'emptiness'. This is the Mahayana teaching that nothing, including ourselves, is anything in and by itself, but that everything is interdependent with everything else. We do not exist separately but as part of a greater whole:

> This is the ultimate meditation which eradicates all our faults, anger, pride, greed, worry, jealousy and eventually leads to enlightenment.

What do you actually do to meditate?

> You sit in a suitable posture such as the lotus position [crosslegged with the feet on opposite thighs] and relax· mind and body. You prepare by reciting the Three Refuges and the Five Precepts. You remember death. You visualise [see in the mind] the various buddhas and bodhisattvas and ask them for help. You generate a good motivation; in other words, like a bodhisattva you are doing this for the sake of all beings rather than yourself. You think of the sufferings of the world until you feel great compassion. That gives you the determination to work towards becoming Buddha in order to help them. You then make your puja offerings [either literally or in the imagination] of flowers, water, incense, etc., confess your faults, rejoice in the happiness of others and ask all the buddhas and bodhisattvas to remain in the world to help. Finally you offer up the universe in the form of a mandala or a special mudra or shape made with the hands. Having made all this preparation, you can go on to meditate. There are two levels. First you think deeply about the meditation topic, then when you develop a very strong feeling, for example of the preciousness of human life, you focus the mind on this feeling so as never to lose it.

Yönten's life is guided by the Ten Virtuous Actions of the Mahayana and the eight vows he took when ordained. The list he gave me of moral guidelines was:

> Not to kill anything, not to steal, no sexual misconduct [for a monk this means celibacy], no false speech, no divisive speech, no idle chatter,

no intoxicants, no malice, no covetousness, no wrong views.

The actual vows that he took were:

> Not to kill, not to steal, no false speech, no eating after midday, not to sit on a high throne or cushion with attachment, no jewellery or adornments, no singing, dancing or playing music with attachment.

In practice this means that he never drinks alcohol, smokes or plays music. It means kindness to all living beings, including slugs and snails. We talked about how we had both spent part of that week rescuing little toads from dangerous roads and had to be extra careful not to step on them, especially in the dark. Once two sheep escaped from a neighbouring farm. As these sheep were about to be sent to the slaughterhouse the community decided to buy them and let them live in the grounds of the centre. They certainly seemed very happy there.

Although when Yönten becomes a gelong he will take over 200 vows, Tibetan Buddhists do not follow the rules slavishly:

> The real rule is compassion. More important than moral vows is the bodhisattva vow to help all beings. So basically what is right is what most helps others.

This may mean bending the rules at times. For example, the vinaya says that monks may not eat after midday, but Yönten eats at 1 p.m. because the lay people in the community find that more convenient. Similarly, the vinaya forbids monks to cook food, but Tibetan monks do join in with the preparation and cooking of food in their monasteries. This ability to judge what is right in certain situations whatever the rules say is called *upaya* or 'skilful means'. It requires both wisdom and love, and is one of the qualities of Buddha.

The Ge lug pa tradition stresses the importance of study as well as meditation. This includes knowledge of the scriptures, the philosophies of teachers of the past and the writings of teachers alive today. Some texts are intellectual and theoretical, others very practical. In Tibet some of the monasteries were like huge universities, with various examinations and degrees of qualification. This tradition is continued in the courses run by the centre.

> My favourite scriptures are the Mahayana sutras, especially the *Prajnaparamita* or 'Perfect Wisdom' which teaches about 'emptiness'. I find it very inspiring. We also study a practical text, written by a lama, called *The Eight Verses of Training the Mind*, which gives eight things to practise, such as not losing control, or helping other people.

Can Yönten sum up Buddhism?

You must remember two things: the law of karma, that is that from good actions comes happiness and from bad actions come unhappiness; secondly, you must remember to benefit others as much as you can.

QUESTIONS

1 *Why do some people get the impression that Buddhism is gloomy and pessimistic? Do you think that this impression is mistaken?*

2 *Why do many Buddhists say that their tradition is not a 'faith' and that faith is not as important in Buddhism as in other religions?*

3 *Why do you think Yönten Gyatso lays so much stress on the importance of faith in Buddhism?*

4 *How would you decide whether a particular teacher or teaching was one to follow?*

5 *Do you agree with Yönten that happiness depends on your own mind rather than on external circumstances?*

6 *Tibetan Buddhist shrines are very colourful, with many statues, symbols and pictures. Some Buddhists meditate in rooms that are completely bare. Can you explain why both of these should be so? Which do you prefer in a place of worship? Which do you prefer in an ordinary room such as your bedroom or a classroom?*

7 *Why do you think Tibetans painted pictures on cloth?*

8 *Do you think it is more important to be kind to others than to keep moral vows? Can you seen any advantages or dangers in the Mahayana idea of upaya?*

9 *What further questions would you like to ask Yönten?*

8

DHARMACHARI TEJANANDA:
spiritual friendship in the city
(Western Buddhist Order)

> The most important single element in my life as a Buddhist has been
> my experience of sangha, friendship and fellowship with other practis-
> ing Buddhists.

The image of a Buddhist as a solitary figure meditating in a cave
could not be further from the truth than in the case of Dharmachari
Tejananda:

> To a member of the Western Buddhist Order, the Buddhist commun-
> ity or sangha is above all one in which you develop 'kalyana mitrata' or
> 'spiritual friendship' with others.

This means that you receive considerable support from others, help
and advice when you need it and the ordinary enjoyment of being
with other people who share your ideals. It is not always easy, for

> True friendship means pointing out to your friend where he or she is
> going wrong.

However, it is invaluable. Order members often live together in
communities and meet regularly. In Bristol the order members meet
for a meal together once a week, and there are regional and national
meetings at weekends once a month. There are also international
meetings every two years.

Tejananda particularly values this experience of Buddhist community and fellowship as he originally tried to practice Buddhism on
his own. He first came across Buddhism through studying it while
training to be a religious studies teacher at college in London.
Originally a Christian, he found Buddhism attractive because

> There is no need for blind belief. Faith in that sense is not a primary
> element in Buddhism. It is not appropriate to call Buddhism a 'faith'; it
> is something you simply put into practice and see for yourself whether
> it works.

At first when he lost his faith in Christianity, Tejananda became an
anarchist:

I was still a strong idealist despite becoming an agnostic. I wanted to change society and make the world a place in which people would relate on a more human level. Pacifism and anarchy seemed to be the way to do this. I thought that if we could rid the world of authority and change social structures life would be great.

However, like many other people, as he grew older he realised that changing the way society is organised does not stop the problem caused by people's greed, hatred and delusion. Buddhism appealed as a more realistic way of making a better world:

I liked the bodhisattva ideal with its emphasis on compassion and working for the welfare of others, and I liked the fact that you don't have to believe in any God.

After leaving college and starting teaching, Tejananda tried to be a Buddhist on his own, teaching himself from books. When he first met the FWBO he realised that this was the Buddhist community that he was looking for. He soon became fully involved and left teaching to move into a residential community in Croydon and help set up and run a vegetarian café and wholefood co-operative. He is now chair of the FWBO Buddhist Centre in Bristol:

We need to be in the city centre to reach people even though a countryside retreat is more conducive to meditation.

Dharmachari Tejananda has been a Buddhist since 1975 and was ordained as a dharmachari or member of the WBO in 1979:

Ordination into the WBO is hard to understand for someone used to the idea of the monk as an ordained Buddhist. For us ordination is the recognition of a genuinely effective commitment to the Three Jewels of Buddhism: the Buddha, the Dharma and the Sangha. It means that the aim of your life is to achieve Buddhahood.

'Dharmachari' means 'one who fares in the Dharma', a really committed Buddhist. This title was introduced by the founder of the WBO, the Venerable Sangharakshita, because the WBO ordinat.ɔn is neither 'monastic' nor 'lay', so that the traditional terms 'bhikkhu' or 'upasaka' were not appropriate. An order member is free to live any lifestyle he or she chooses – monk, nun or lay, married or single. Yet, according to Tejananda, the level of commitment is much deeper than that of the average layperson in a Buddhist country, who calls him/herself a Buddhist and takes the Three Refuges largely as a part of his or her culture and nationality, and also probably much deeper than the person from a Buddhist background who takes temporary ordination as a monk or nun out of traditional custom. For the WBO, the sangha does not mean the community of monks, but the community of really effective Buddhists.

Dharmachari Tejananda was ordained by Sangharakshita. After a few months of involvement with the FWBO he asked to become a *mitra* or friend of the order. A year or so later he requested ordination, and after a further year and a half Sangharakshita and other senior order members felt he was ready and his ordination took place on a short retreat (ordination for men now usually involves a three-month course in Spain). The actual ceremony is in two parts. The first is a private ceremony with Sangharakshita or another senior order member where you offer flowers, incense and light and recite the Three Refuges and the Five Precepts in Pali. You are given a particular bodhisattva to mediate upon using the *visualisation* technique, and a particular mantra associated with that bodhisattva to chant. This practise involves trying to see in the mind the bodhisattva who represents your goal of enlightenment. Tejananda's particular bodhisattva is Manjusri, the personification of wisdom. You also receive a new name to symbolise your new life. Tejananda means 'fiery or incandescent bliss'.

> This private ceremony signifies your individual personal determination to go for refuge.

Then follows a public ceremony at which the candidates are sprinkled with water, symbolising purification, their new names are announced and they are given the kesa.

> This ceremony signifies full acceptance into the WBO sangha.

The kesa is a small white stole which originally symbolised a monk's robe. The idea comes from Japanese Buddhism. The kesa is embroidered with the emblem of the WBO which shows the Three Jewels of Buddhism: gold for the Buddha, blue for the Dharma and red for the Sangha. The Three Jewels rest on a moon (symbol of purity) and a lotus flower (symbol of love).

> We wear the kesa for puja, or for teaching classes, or whenever we need to be identified as a Buddhist.

A typical day for Dharmachari Tejananda starts with meditation. The rest of the day might be spent answering letters and in other administrative tasks, preparing lectures and talks, writing articles for

FWBO publications and visiting 'spiritual friends'. Most evenings are taken up with classes on Buddhism and meditation, for both beginners and more experienced Buddhists. The classes are the centre's main source of income.

The meditations practised in the FWBO are of two basic kinds, meditation on breathing and meditation on love or *metta*:

> Mindfulness of breathing enables you to be more aware, and metta helps you to be more sympathetic to other people. For order members there is the additional practice of visualisation of our chosen bodhisatt-va, which inspires us with the ideal we are trying to embody.

Meditation on metta or loving kindness proceeds like this. In a meditation posture (e.g. on a chair, sitting upright) you try to encourage positive feelings of friendship and love, wishing well to all beings. You start with yourself, feeling positive about yourself, accepting yourself and hoping things go well for you: 'May I be well and happy.' Then you try to extend this feeling to someone you like, such as a close friend of the same sex, hoping that all goes well for them. The feeling is then extended to someone that you feel neutral about, perhaps someone that you have met but do not know very well. After this you try to extend the same feelings towards someone that you do not like, or someone with whom you have problems. Finally the feeling is imagined as extended out to every living being in the universe. The procedure can be repeated with the feelings of compassion, joy and even-mindedness, or seeing everyone as equal. This is a traditional meditation practised by most Buddhist traditions, but particularly emphasised in the FWBO.

Every Thursday evening at the centre there is puja in the shrine room. The shrine contains a central statue of Buddha Shakyamuni, two carved wooden stupas, candles, flowers and the seven bowls for offerings traditional in Mahayana Buddhism. There is also a carved wooden skull and a bell. The puja ceremony follows a special text called the Sevenfold Puja, put together by Sangharakshita from a famous Mahayana text. This puja is mostly in English with some chanting in Pali and mantras in Sankskrit, the language in which many of the Mahayana were first composed. The puja involves offering flowers, chanting 'om mani padme hum' (the mantra of Avalokitesvara), saluting the buddhas and bodhisattvas, taking the Three Refuges and Five Precepts in Pali, confessing faults and resolving not to commit them again, rejoicing in the good deeds of all beings, asking the buddhas and bodhisattvas to remain in the world, repeating the short Mahayana sutra called the Heart Sutra on the theme of 'emptiness', and finally transferring the merit or good karma from this ceremony to all beings rather than just keeping it to oneself.

There are other devotions in the puja book. There is a selection of mantras for the different buddhas and bodhisattvas, a ceremony for dedicating a special place or shrine, blessings from the Pali scriptures (as used in Theravada pirit ceremonies) and a devotion to the three jewels. The FWBO has ceremonies of blessing for new babies and for funerals. Marriage blessings, more common in India, are rare in this country and marriage is seen as a private affair:

> From the Buddhist point of view, people don't have to go through any ceremony at all to be married. To live as though married is to be married.

Although some order members and many 'friends' are married and have families, Tejananda considers that the present Western form of marriage and the small 'nuclear family' are

> an expression of a not too healthy society. The traditional extended family is perhaps psychologically healthier in some ways.

The FWBO celebrates a series of festivals. Buddha Day in May resembles Wesak but celebrates only Buddha's enlightenment, not his birth or death. Dharma Day in July is also based on traditional celebrations of the Buddha's first sermon. Sangha Day in October replaces the Theravada kathina ceremony. Buddha's birthday is celebrated on 8 April as in Japan and his death on 19 February. They also celebrate Padmasambhava Day in July (Padmasambhava was an enlightened Indian teacher who first established Buddhism in Tibet and is particularly revered by the Nying ma pa tradition of Tibetan Buddhism), and the founding of the WBO and the FWBO on 6 and 7 April respectively. For ordinary puja the offering bowls on the shrine are filled with water. For festivals the bowls are filled with the real offerings – food, flowers and so on.

The Ten Moral Precepts taken by WBO members are:

> Not to harm living things, not to steal, no sexual misconduct, no false speech, no harsh speech, no useless speech, no slanderous speech, no covetousness, no animosity, no false views.
> They are balanced by Ten Positive Precepts:

> Loving-kindness, open-handed giving, contentment, truthful speech, kind speech, helpful speech, generosity, love and wisdom.
> There is no fixed hard line on moral issues, but Buddhism gives you guidance on everything, whether the ecological crisis or nuclear weapons.

In practice most order members are vegetarian, and few smoke or drink:

> Personally that is no hardship. The average pub atmosphere is not a pleasant experience. However, I'm not a teetotaller.

Although abortion is killing, there may be circumstances where it might be the most 'skilful' course of action.

With sexual relationships the important thing is that they should be positive, healthy and 'skilful':

> We don't expect people to repress their sexuality. There is no ethical difference between being formally married and 'living together', or being heterosexual and being gay.

Many order members have found that the lifestyle that suits them best is living in single-sex communities:

> This is not sexist because women and men are equal in the WBO. However, we have found that men and women do things differently. For example, women seem to take longer to become ready for ordination. In our society women are often dominated by the male point of view. Women need to discover themselves separate from men.

However, there is nothing to stop anyone living as a couple, married or unmarried, or living alone as Dharmachari Tejananda does at present.

On controversial moral issues

> what is needed is not protest but a change in consciousness. Being a Buddhist is part of the answer to problems like the threat of nuclear war and the ecological crisis.

Although Buddhists tend to stress inner change rather than campaigning to change the world, like other Buddhist groups the FWBO is also active in providing practical help. One example is its charity, 'Aid for India', which works with ex-untouchables in that country and also provides relief in times of trouble like flood, drought and famine. Buddhist morality should affect your everday life:

> For example, you should drive your car with awareness and consideration of the potential effects of what you are doing, with patience and courtesy towards other road users.

As Tejananda gave up teaching, is he critical of the education system?

I'm personally unhappy with the school system. Some Buddhist parents choose to send their children to Steiner schools rather than state schools because they feel there is a more human approach.

How does Tejananda understand the buddhas and bodhisattvas?

The Buddha embodies the ideal of enlightenment that all human beings can achieve, the fact that we can all grow infinitely beyond our present state. The so-called 'archetypal' bodhisattvas [the famous ones of whom there are images] can be seen as embodying different aspects or facets of enlightenment. The actual figures probably emerged from 'visions' experienced in meditation. When we 'visualise' them it is as if we 'project' in front of us our own potential state of enlightenment in an idealised human form. However, they can in a sense be seen as 'really' existing in that they are aspects of enlightenment which is a reality, in so far as living beings realise it. When the bodhisattvas are visualised in meditation they are always finally dissolved into 'emptiness' so that we don't fall into the trap of taking them literally. The figure of Manjusri is a human creation, but the wisdom of enlightenment is real.

Among the historical figures revered are Padmasambhava and Milarepa, two enlightened people of special importance to the Tibetans. The present leader of the WBO and FWBO is the founder of the movement, Sangharakshita, who until recently ordained all the order members. Will there be a successor when he dies?

No, not a single person. Various senior order members will fulfil collectively his current role.

QUESTIONS

1 *Why do you think Tejananda wanted to stress the importance of community and friendhsip in Buddhism?*

2 *Why does he claim that Buddhism is not a 'faith'? Does this contradict what Yönten Gyatso said about faith?*

3 *Some Buddhists live in forest retreats, others in city centres. What are the advantages and disadvantages of each as far as practising Buddhism is concerned?*

4 *Why do you think many people involved with the FWBO have started businesses with others similarly involved rather than con-*

tinuing with their previous jobs? Why have these often been co-operatives? Why was a vegetarian café and a wholefood co-operative chosen?

5 *Why do you think WBO members prefer not to wear a robe or shave their heads?*

6 *Why do you think they have the kesa?*

7 *What is the point of an exercise like the meditation on metta?*

8 *Why do you think that for this meditation it is suggested you think of a best friend rather than a boy/girlfriend or close relation?*

9 *Why do you think there is a wooden skull on the shrine?*

10 *Why do you think the puja is mostly in English? Why do you think that some Pali recitations and Sanskrit mantras are retained?*

11 *Why is there no marriage ceremony? Do you agree that marriage really has nothing to do with religion? Why do you think Tejananda considers that the 'nuclear' family can be psychologically unhealthy?*

12 *In FWBO practice, elements from Theravada Buddhism, Tibetan Buddhism and Japanese Buddhism are mixed. Why did Sangharakshita decide to do this? Can you pick out which is which?*

13 *Why do you think the FWBO emphasises the list of positive precepts as well as the more familiar negative ones?*

14 *What are the advantages and disadvantages of single-sex communities such as schools?*

15 *Why do you think the experience of the WBO has been that women take longer to feel ready for ordination?*

16 *What features of the education system and of schools in Britain do you think Buddhists might dislike?*

17 *What difference do you think it makes that the majority of British Buddhists are converts from ethnically British backgrounds rather than being from families whose origins are in Buddhist countries and culture?*

18 *Are there any questions you would like to ask Dharmachari Tejananda?*

9

VICKY ABEL:
world peace by the year 2000 (Nichiren Shoshu)

Vicky Abel is married and has three children aged 15, 9 and 7. She works part time for a charity that helps victims of crime in Bristol. She has been a Nichiren Shoshu Buddhist since 1975. Her younger children are happy to join in the chanting and to call themselves Buddhists. They attend a local school and are quite happy to participate in Christian assemblies as well. Vicky's eldest daughter practises regularly.

Vicky learnt of Nichiren Shoshu Buddhism through her sister who met a Japanese businessman when working as a waitress in London. This man introduced Vicky's sister to the chanting because he noticed that she was very unhappy. What attracted Vicky herself to Buddhism?

> I liked the sound of the chanting. I liked the way that there were no secrets and that no one asked for any money. I saw an extraordinary change in my sister. Most of all I liked the people I met. They were open, laughing, enjoying themselves and were wonderful friends.
>
> The real aim of our practice is to reveal Buddhahood in ourselves and establish world peace. By the year 2000 we hope to see a definite indication of the reversal of the very negative path that the human race is going along.

The practice of Nichiren Shoshu Buddhism is relatively simple. It involves the daily chanting of a Japanese mantra or short phrase. As well as drawing out one's potential Buddhahood and bringing about world peace, regular chanting is claimed to achieve impressive practical results in one's own life:

> Wonderful things happen. You can chant for whatever you desire – money, a new car, a house, a job. It cures illnesses, mends marriages and produces babies . . . It has helped me with my relationships, which are after all the most important part of our lives, and since I've been chanting about my work, the crime rate in Bristol has gone down!

It is based on a profound Buddhist philosophy which explains that chanting puts you in tune with the rhythm of the universe, the state of Buddahood where everything functions harmoniously and correctly for everybody's happiness:

It does not work by magic, but by changing the quality of our lives, so that we manifest Buddhahood and make the best of our lives.

However, it does not matter whether you understand how it works; all that matters is actually to do the practice and results will be seen:

After all, you don't need to know the chemical constituents of water to quench your thirst with it!

Chanting can be used to achieve any aim, no matter how materialistic or even selfish. Vicky once met a drug dealer who had chanted for success in his business. Surely Buddhism is not about satisfying our selfish desires for material things and worldly success? In the Four Noble Truths the Buddha claimed that desire or selfish craving was the cause of all our suffering.

Yes, the real aim of the practice is to achieve Buddhahood. However, receiving material benefits is an encouragement. If you recall the life story of Shakyamuni Buddha, he wanted to help people with their real-life problems of illness, old age and death. It is not desires that are wrong, but attachment to desires. Rather than suppressing desires you should use your desires as a catalyst towards enlightenment.

Though your chanting may start off with a selfish intention, the practice brings out the wisdom and compassion within you, and you will naturally become less selfish. In the case of the drug dealer, his business did go well, but he began to see how wrong this way of life was and gave it up.

The practice of chanting means that for 30–40 minutes each morning and 20–30 minutes each evening Vicky and her family will perform what is known as *gongyo*. This means reciting in Japanese two chapters of the Mahayana sutra called the *Lotus Sutra*, chanting the mantra 'namo myoho rengye kyo' and offering silent prayers for world peace and other intentions. You make your resolutions for the day ahead, and express gratitude to the universe for your life. The practice purifies the mind and sets your life on a harmonious path. The two chapters from the Lotus Sutra are the ones in which the central messages of the scripture are announced. In chapter 2 the Buddha Shakyamuni reveals the hitherto unknown secret that all beings shall become buddhas, equal in status to himself. In chapter 16 he reveals that his historical life was a form of pretence. In reality, he has been enlightened from all eternity, and comes into existence age after age in order to help beings. The earlier Buddhist teachings, such as the scriptures followed by the Theravada Buddhists, and the impression given of his birth, enlightenment and death, were examples of upaya, bending the strict truth for the sake of helping people. Some would only be attracted by the earlier teachings, and some would not get on with the practice if they knew the Buddha was eternal. These truths are illustrated with parables. The Buddha is compared to a father promising his children all sorts of toys to get them out of a burning house, and to a doctor who pretended to die in order to make his sons take their medicine.

Although Nichiren Buddhism is based on these teachings, the Lotus Sutra is not studied in detail because

> It is hard to understand and open to misinterpretation.

The two chapters are simply recited; knowing the meaning of every word is not important:

> The actual recitation, the sound vibration, changes something within ourselves.

This applies also to the mantra 'Namo myoho rengye kyo':

> Literally it means 'hail to the mystic law of the lotus flower', which is the full title of the Lotus Sutra. You are not honouring the Lotus Sutra as a book, but the teaching contained within it.

There is a lot of deep symbolism in this mantra. *Myoho*, the mystic law, refers to the law of the universe, that is both the law of karma and the secret of the Buddhahood of all. *Myo* and *ho* taken separately mean 'life' and 'death', and so refer to the energy that brings rebirth from death. *Rengye*, the lotus flower, is the only flower that bears flowers and seed pods at the same time:

> This symbolises the simultaneity of cause and effect; everything we do has an instant effect.

Lotus flowers also bloom in muddy swamps and are a traditional Buddhist symbol for the potential beauty of human lives despite the mess they are in. 'Kyo' means 'sound' or 'teaching':

> In Buddhism teaching is by voice, and sound vibration is very important.

A possible translation of the mantra according to Vicky is:

> I devote my life to the law of the universe, which is cause and effect.

In order for the chanting to 'work', you must concentrate hard on the mantra and not let the mind wander into daydream. To help with this a set of 108 beads called *juzu* is held in the hand and the beads are rubbed together occasionally to make a noise. The circle of beads has five short extensions which make it look like a human body, with a head, arms and legs.

The chanting takes place in front of a shrine of *Butsu dan*, 'Buddha place'. Vicky uses her front room as a shrine room. It is painted in pale colours and feels peaceful. The shrine itself consists of a large wooden cabinet. In the centre, behind the doors of the cabinet, is the *gohonzon*. This is a scroll inscribed with Chinese characters, including those for 'namo myoho rengye kyo' and the name 'Nichiren'. A gohonzon is given to everyone who joins Nichiren Shoshu, and must be treated with great respect (including not being photographed) and sent back to the head temple when you die. There is a special ceremony in which the high priest of Nichiren Shoshu inscribes the scroll. As there are now millions of followers, the priest does not inscribe all the scrolls by hand; instead they are printed from a wooden block. The gohonzon represents Buddha-hood and the law of the universe, and reflects your own potential:

> Chanting to the gohonzon brings out Buddhahood; the person who inscribed it was in a state of Buddhahood.

Among the items on the shrine are the usual offerings of flowers, candles for light, incense to purify the air, and fruit. Fresh water is offered every day:

> These are our offerings to life.

There are also two vases of evergreen leaves to symbolise eternity and two statues of crane birds to symbolise good fortune. There is a gong for use in chanting and a prayer for peace in Northern Ireland. There is no statue of the Buddha:

> If you have a statue of the Buddha it implies that you worship him. He is not a god, just a human being. We don't worship him but the thing that makes him a buddha, Buddhahood, life at its greatest potential. Buddha is not a person but a state of life, when everything functions harmoniously and correctly for the happiness of all. To talk of 'the' Buddha, or 'a' buddha, or to have a statue, will give the wrong impression that Buddhahood is removed and apart from the world. There is not 'the Buddha' like 'God' over against the universe. The Buddha is ourselves.

Nichiren Shoshu Buddhism originates with the teaching of a

thirteenth-century Japanese monk who called himself 'Nichiren' or 'sun-lotus'. He attributed all the troubles of his time – war, disease, drought, corruption – to the fact that people were following mistaken forms of Buddhism. Nichiren came from the *Tendai* tradition of Buddhism, founded in Japan in the eighth century by *Dengyo Daishi*. Tendai respected all Buddhist scriptures but taught that the final, supreme teaching of the Buddha was the Lotus Sutra. The philosophy of this scripture teaches that all things are interdependent, not as parts of a greater whole but in the sense that the totality of the universe, Buddhahood, is present in every individual, even every grain of dust. Nichiren called people back to the Lotus Sutra and its teaching. He inscribed gohonzons and taught the mantra of the Lotus Sutra. Nichiren is looked upon as the true Buddha, equal in status to Shakyamuni:

> He represents the eternity of Buddhahood. He is the only person who revealed a way for ordinary people to obtain enlightenment in this lifetime.

Nichiren taught that all other forms of Buddhism were wrong because they were based on teachings of the Buddha that were only provisional until the full truth of the Lotus Sutra. He was very direct and forceful in his teaching and was persecuted both by rulers and by Buddhist leaders, but he gained popularity when his chanting was said to have turned back the invading Mongol army.

The organisation to which Vicky belongs, Nichiren Shoshu UK, is part of a lay organisation for Nichiren Shoshu Buddhists known in Japan as *Soka Gakkai*, the 'Society for Creating Values'. This movement was founded in 1932 and has become very popular since the introduction of religious freedom in Japan at the end of the Second World War. Its positive approach appealed to people who had to rebuild lives shattered by the war:

> It was called 'the cripples' religion' because it attracted those with terrible problems.

Soka Gakkai has grown to include about 10 per cent of Japan's population, around 8 million people. It is very well organised with large financial resources. Schools and universities have been built in Japan by the movement, as well as a huge new temple at the foot of Mount Fuji, which houses the original 2 m gohonzon inscribed by Nichiren himself. There is also a political party associated with the movement. Mr Ikeda, the president of Soka Gakkai, meets with world leaders and has been awarded a United Nations medal for his peace efforts. There have been some criticisms of Soka Gakkai for being too aggressive, too materialistic and having too much money:

> Maybe some of the early members were overzealous because of the urgent needs of post-war Japan. However, our sheer success has led to a lot of false rumours and bad press.

Nichiren Shoshu UK, on the other hand, is certainly not aggressive in its approach and Vicky described it as growing slowly but steadily. It is highly organised, based on a hierarchy of groups, districts, chapters and regions, with separate groups for men, women, young men and young women. Vicky is general chapter leader for Wiltshire, Somerset, Avon and Gloucestershire. She will be involved in meetings two or three times a week. There are not temples or priests in the UK and people meet in houses.

There are ceremonies for joining Nichiran Shoshu, for funerals and for marriage. The ceremony for joining is called *gojukai* and must be performed by a priest. You are touched with a rolled-up gohonzon and given your own gohonzon to keep. You recite gongyo and make promises to practise properly and not to follow any other religion. Children can receive gojukai and Vicky's children did when they were babies.

Marriages and funerals are conducted by approved lay people. Vicky was married in a Buddhist ceremony in front of the gohonzon. Gongyo is recited and the couple drink three cups of sake (Japanese rice wine) from three different-sized cups:

> These represent your cup of happiness . . . the last cup is quite large . . . you can feel the effects of the alcohol by the end of the ceremony!
> Funerals are joyful because we believe in rebirth and chant gongyo to give the dead person the best possible start in their new life.

The Japanese priesthood is quite small. The priests are family men, not monks, and their function is to preserve the tradition handed down from Nichiren. The high priest inscribes the gohonzons and performs a special ceremony for world peace. Vicky witnessed this when she went on a pilgrimage to the main temple in Japan:

> It was so powerful. For 700 years, every morning between 2 a.m. and 4 a.m. the high priest chants for world peace. He was absolutely concentrated. You could really feel the vibrations going out into the universe.

There are no women priests, but there is no particular law forbidding women to be priests.

There is no list of moral precepts for Nichiren Shoshu Buddhists. You are expected to do the practice and to keep the laws of your country. Apart from that

> There are no restrictions on the way you live your life. You can do what you want.

Vicky's family eat meat and think that it is morally acceptable to do so if you respect the life that has been given for yours. She drinks alcohol, goes to pubs, and enjoys the things that most people enjoy:

> If you really want world peace it is important to be in society rather than being 'holier than thou' on a mountain.

Issues such as whether to have an abortion or to work on nuclear projects for the Ministry of Defence, as Vicky's husband has done in the past, are for the individual to decide. However, as you practise Buddhism, you find that you act in a moral way naturally rather than as a result of rules. You become very conscious of karma, 'the universal law of cause and effect'. There is no point in acting immorally because you will only suffer yourself in the end. If you are dishonest with money – dodging bus fares or keeping the extra money when given too much change in a shop – you will eventually lose your own good fortune:

> As you practise, the gap between cause and effect seems to shorten. You can see clearly what your actions lead to. We tend to blame others for our sufferings, but Buddhism makes you take responsibility for your own life.

At a deeper level, according to the Tendai philosophy, all things are connected, the whole universe is present in each individual, so that what you do affects others:

> The saying is that there are 3,000 worlds in a single life-moment. In a sense that is difficult to explain. All things are one. This means that every action you take affects the whole universe. This certainly makes you take your actions seriously.

Vicky believes strongly in rebirth:

> Our life cannot possibly be just this one short period. It makes absolute sense to me. Otherwise why should children be born in such different circumstances? Life would be totally unfair.

Belief in karma seems to make sense only if you also believe in rebirth. Why else would children be born in such different circumstances? Rebirth cannot be proved objectively, but

> You can prove it to your own satisfaction. I have lived my life based on these beliefs and my life has improved.

The goal throughout these lives is to reveal Buddhahood. There is no end point, however, when the goal is reached and you

> float off on a pink cloud.

Those who reveal Buddhahood are bodhisattvas whose function is to help others and who therefore choose to be reborn in this sort of world:

> Enlightenment means making the best of your life, being happy and making other people happy.

Vicky looks forward to eternal rebirth rather than a 'pink cloud' heaven:

> It would be boring otherwise.

QUESTIONS

1 *Look up the Four Noble Truths and see what Buddha said about desire. What do you think Vicky means when she says it is not desires that are wrong, but attachment to desires?*

2 *Do Buddhists from other traditions ever use their religious ceremonies to achieve worldly benefits?*

3 *Why do you think the recitation is performed in Japanese?*

4 *What three main teachings would you identify as being recalled in gongyo? How would this regular practice affect your life during the rest of the day?*

5 *Why do you think photographing the gohonzon is not allowed?*

6 *Why is Nichiren often said to be untypical of the Buddhist approach to religious practices?*

7 *What do you think would appeal to people with problems in the Nichiren Shoshu tradition?*

8 *What else would you like to ask Vicky?*

10

JUNTOKU DEGUCHI:
harmony and tolerance (Japanese Wa Shu)

Mr Juntoku Deguchi is headmaster of the Shi Tennoji Japanese school in Suffolk; he is also a Buddhist priest of the *Wa Shu* sect of Buddhism and an architect who has designed, among other things, the beautiful new temple, gardens and tea house in the school grounds. Before coming to Britain three and a half years ago, he taught at a Japanese university and was a director of the Shi Tennoji Foundation, a Buddhist educational organisation.

Mr Deguchi came to Britain to set up the school, which opened in 1986. At present there are 246 students aged between 8 and 18. They may be children of Japanese parents, working in Britain or elsewhere in Europe, or they may be sent from Japan in order to learn English and become familiar with Western ways. The aim of the school is to create understanding between the two nations and cultures:

> Students are given the opportunity to learn about Western culture as well as learn the language, and Western people have the opportunity to learn about Japanese culture.

The school is very involved in the local community. Students from the school have spent time in the local schools, and children from local schools visit the Shi Tennoji school. One local primary teacher I spoke to was very enthusiastic about this. His class of nine-year-olds had thoroughly enjoyed their visit to the school, trying on Japanese clothes, eating Japanese food and learning Japanese games. The Japanese children in their traditional dress make a wonderful addition to local carnival processions.

Local people are welcome to visit the school, and a small group attends weekly meditation sessions on Wednesday evenings. The meditation practised is sitting meditation, very similar to zazen meditation, in which the mind is calmed through concentrating on breathing and the thoughts that arise. While I was at the school, I joined six local people for a 45-minute session of meditation, facing the bare wooden walls of the archery hall. The session ended with Mr Deguchi leading the group in the chanting of the Buddhist scripture called the 'Heart Sutra', which teaches that all things are 'empty' – that is, that things are nothing in and by themselves. The sound of the chanting, on one low note, filled the room and created a very still atmosphere.

As well as learning about Western culture, the school pupils maintain their own culture and traditions. Most of the children are from Buddhist families and the school is run on Buddhist principles. In what way is a Buddhist school different from other schools? The obvious outward difference is that, whereas a Christian school would have Christian hymns and prayers, in this school morning assembly means the chanting of Buddhist scriptures. The students practise meditation on Sunday evening, and before every lesson there is a brief session of meditation lasting one or two minutes. However, Buddhist education is not just chanting scriptures and meditating; it means

> concentrating on your work and working hard.

It is also about respect for others, and living in peace and harmony with others. Buddhism is

> a different attitude to life, with different goals and different values.

What Mt Deguchi valued most about his own Buddhist upbringing was that

> Buddhism teaches you that wealth and status are not the most important things in life, not the things that you should pursue.

He felt that both Japanese and British people tended to be too materialistic, looking for happiness in the wrong place. If you should not aim for money and status, what should be your goal in life?

> To know yourself, to be enlightened.

Everyone has the potential for enlightenment within them:

> Buddha means perfect being, someone with no worries, peaceful, natural, a calm state of mind.

However, it is not easy to explain Buddhism – and not because we were working through a translator:

> You cannot understand it by reading books or thinking about it; you have to practise yourself by sitting in meditation and understanding through experience.

Thus a Buddhist education does not mean indoctrination or forcing a religion upon reluctant teenagers. It means living in a community run on Buddhist principles. Mr Deguchi felt that it was difficult for teenagers to be very interested in religion,

> But the contact with Buddhism might pay off in later life.

Mr Deguchi was ordained as a Buddhist priest at the age of ten. His father was also a priest and he and his family lived in the Shi Tennoji temple in Osaka in Japan, together with four other families. He has now been a priest for 40 years. The ordination ceremony involves making vows before your immediate superior in the priest-hood. The vows included promising:

> Not to lie, not to be jealous, to have sympathy for others, to be moral in sexual matters, not to steal, not to kill, not to drink too much, to be generous, and a lot more.

In this list I recognised the basic Five Precepts of Buddhism.

> The most important precept is not to kill, therefore war is always wrong.

Japanese Buddhists generally do not take this precept as ruling what they eat.

At ordination your head is shaved and you receive the robes. Mr Deguchi wears a black robe and kesa or stole embroidered with gold. His hair is worn very short and he has a short beard, now greying. He does not wear his ceremonial robes all the time – during the day he wore his work clothes of loose, oatmeal-coloured pyjamas. Sometimes he looks very solemn and serious, and at other times he breaks into a broad grin, a smile full of warmth that extends to his twinkling eyes.

Mr Deguchi is married and has four children. Japanese Buddhist clergy are usually married, unlike the traditional monk of Theravada and of most Tibetan Buddhism. His youngest child is 14 and attends a local school rather than the Shi Tennoji school. This is not just because the family are now settled in Britain, but because

> It would not be fair to the other children here at the school, who do not have their parents with them.

Mr Deguchi sees no difficulty in his daughter, his wife and himself continuing to practise Buddhism in this country:

> Buddhism spread from India to China and then Japan; there is no reason why it should not spread to Britain.

Buddhism can adapt to different cultures, and is not tied down to any one culture of nationality. However, although Buddhism is spreading to Britain and Mr Deguchi welcomes British people to his meditation classes, he does not see himself as having a mission to convert Britain to Buddhism:

> It is not my intention to wipe out other religions and make everyone into Buddhists. Rather we must all accept that there are many different religions and learn to understand and accept each other. This is the way to bring peace into the world and avoid conflict and war.

The particular tradition of Buddhism followed by Mr Deguchi is called Wa Shu. *Shu* is Japanese for a religious group or sect and *Wa* means harmony. The Wa Shu traces its history back to the first introduction of Buddhism into Japan, before Buddhism there split up into the different sects of Zen, Pure Land and so on. Thus Wa Shu sees itself as a non-sectarian form of Buddhism in which people of all sects are welcome. The sect reveres Prince Shotoku (574–622) who first made Buddhism the religion of Japan. Prince Shotoku, who also introduced many other aspects of Chinese culture into Japan, is looked upon as a great statesman and a saint. Indeed, for the Wa Shu his statue replaces that of a buddha or bodhisattva on the temple shrine:

> For us Japanese he is Buddha, as he brought the teachings of Buddhism to Japan.

Mr Deguchi stressed that the statue was a focus for meditation, rather as Theravada Buddhists view a statue of Buddha Shakyamuni. However, Mrs Deguchi admitted that people would also pray to Prince Shotoku when in need of help, as people do to gods, saints and bodhisattvas in other traditions:

> For instance, if going on a journey, I might pray that the car would not crash, or if one of the children had an examination, I might pray that they do well.

In addition to the statue of Prince Shotoku, the huge wooden temple contained statues of Shi Tennoji, the 'four heavenly kings' after whom the school is named. The four heavenly kings are four 'guardian gods' of Buddhism, protecting the four quarters of the universe, north, south, east and west. These traditional figures were brought to Japan from China and were based originally on Hindu gods. Buddhism has never asked people to give up their traditional gods, only to see the superiority of the Buddhist way, and many local gods are found in Buddhist temples all over the world.

The Shi Tennoji school is named after the Shi Tennoji temple in Osaka, Japan, where Mr Deguchi was brought up. This famous temple was originally built by Prince Shotoku in 593 and was dedicated to the 'four guardian gods' who were protecting the spread of Buddhism in Japan. The temple originally functioned not only as a place of worship, but also as a free hospital and dispensary of medicinal herbs, a shelter for the poor and homeless and a centre for Buddhist education, including philosophy, science and arts as well as religious education. This practicality was typical of the Buddhism established by Prince Shotoku, who stressed the virtues of tolerance and compassion. Buddhism should mean working for the benefit of others, the bodhisattva ideal, and thus should build up a compassionate society. There should be tolerance of conflicting viewpoints, and so all traditions of Buddhism were welcomed as well as other religions like Confucianism and Shinto. Buddhism was made the state religion of Japan in 594 and, although this did not continue to be the case throughout Japanese history, the social and institutional, and ritual and ceremonial dimensions of Buddhism have always been important in Japan.

After the time of Prince Shotoku, Buddhism began to form different sects, following different scriptures and teachers. The sect closest in attitude to Prince Shotoku was the Tendai sect founded by Dengyo Daishi (767–822). This sect welcomed all forms of Buddhist teaching and practice as different paths to the same goal. The scripture most revered by Tendai was the Lotus Sutra, which teaches that all have the potential to be buddhas and that, while the eternal Buddha introduced different forms of Buddhism to suit different sorts of people, in reality all ways are one. Dengyo Daishi established the famous Tendai monastery at Mt Hiei, where many famous Japanese monks started their training. Mr Deguchi also spent some time training in this monastery. The Shi Tennoji temple was affiliated to the Tendai sect in 1010 and remained Tendai until 1949 when the temple decided to return to the original non-sectarian Wa Shu of Prince Shotoku.

As a priest, Mr Deguchi is involved in daily ceremonies and ceremonies for birth, marriage and death. As in other forms of Buddhism, the funeral ceremony is considered the most important. The funeral ceremony follows the pattern of the ordination ceremony, so that anyone who is not a priest is ordained at death. The body will then be cremated. When asked what happens to those who die, Mr Deguchi replied:

> Buddhism does not ask the question what happens after death. It is not something to worry about.

I received the impression that Buddhism was something for this life, that enlightenment could be found in the present. Yet

> It is not true that there is nothing after death.

It is just not worth wasting time thinking about it. When asked about rebirth, Mr Deguchi said:

> People are free to think about it.

Mr Deguchi was returning to Japan at the end of the week, to conduct ceremonies for the summer festival of *Obon* on 15 August. It is traditional to return home for this festival at which Buddhists pray for their ancestors. The festival is connected with a story about one of Shakyamuni Buddha's disciples who discovered that his mother was suffering rebirth in a hell world. Out of compassion the Buddha arranged for her release. Thus Buddhists hope that prayers and offerings will help their dead relatives towards a better rebirth or nirvana. People visit the graves of their ancestors and pray for the dead. However, it is not a gloomy time, but a joyful occasion when living families get back together, and villages organise summer fêtes and dancing.

The dead are remembered on two other occasions in the year: the spring and autumn equinoxes (21 March and 21 September). People will visit the temple and graves of their ancestors. One custom is to write the names of ancestors on a piece of wood and let it float away on the river. This symbolises the journey of life, the fact that death is natural and the need to 'let go'. The name of this festival is *Higan*, 'the other shore', the enlightenment towards which we are all heading. The equinox is an important turning point in nature, a time of balance between winter and summer.

New Year is also celebrated, on 31 December and 1 January. Celebrations last for 14 days. In the Shi Tennoji temple there is a traditional custom where boys compete for possession of an ancient 'lucky charm', a brief Buddhist scripture written on a piece of paper and stuck into a willow branch. It is said that if this is put in a field it will ensure a good crop, or if put on board a ship will ensure a good catch of fish.

The most important festival for the Wa Shu sect is on 22 February in commemoration of the death of Prince Shotoku. He is also remembered on the twenty-second day of each month.

While I was visiting the school, I was invited to join in a tea ceremony. The Cha-do or 'way of tea' was developed in fifteenth-century Japan, at a time of wars and political troubles. The idea is to create harmony and tranquillity among the guests invited to the ceremony. The ceremony took place in a specially designed tea house, a small, very simple and very beautiful wooden building. The floor is covered in tatami – simple straw matting – and the walls are bare apart from a simple scroll of calligraphy. As it was a warm evening, the windows were opened on to a view of the beautiful Japanese gardens and the sound of the waterfall and birdsongs. The green tea was carefully prepared by Mrs Deguchi, dressed in a beautiful traditional kimono and using traditional implements.

The ceremony follows a slow, careful ritual pattern. One by one the guests are offered a bowl of tea. Respect for each other is shown by bowing when offering and receiving tea, and the custom is for the person receiving the bowl to offer it first to the people sitting on his or her left or right. When these decline with a bow, the bowl of tea is accepted and drunk with mindfulness and respect. The bowl is then turned in the hands and the beauty of its design admired. Although everything takes place in a ceremonial fashion, there is no tension about getting everything right; rather the atmosphere is very re-laxed. We made gentle conversation and there were a lot of smiles and laughter. We also received Japanese sweets, carefully wrapped in paper packets, to eat with the tea and to take home.

The aim of the tea ceremony is to create a tranquil, peaceful atmosphere, where mind and body are calmed and where, by concentrating on the making and taking of tea, one lives totally in the present, leaving past and future worries behind. A sense of harmony and respect is created between the people present and with the natural world. Thus taking tea becomes a form of meditation. I certainly found it a peaceful, beautiful and enjoyable experience.

The same aim can be achieved through other art forms such as calligraphy and flower arranging, or through martial arts such as kyodo (archery). These are also practised at the school. The combination of ceremonial correctness and complete naturalness is particular associated with Zen Buddhism, but this 'disciplined casualness' is found in many aspects of Japanese society.

The Japanese 'Zen' garden recently laid out in the school grounds captured the same spirit of precise planning which achieves a completely natural effect. The little stream, pond and waterfall, and the natural stones, looking as if they just happened to be there rather than having been placed there, create a very peaceful calming effect.

In the garden and in the tea ceremony, it was possible to feel something of the peace, harmony and tolerance that Mr Deguchi is hoping the Shi Tennoji school will help to create between the Japanese and European cultures, and a hint of the eternal peace and harmony, wisdom and compassion that is the aim of Buddhism, and which in Japanese Buddhist thought could be seen in the here and now, if only we knew how to look.

QUESTIONS

1 *Why do you think traditional buildings like the temple, meditation room and tea house are built with plain wooden walls and have little decoration?*

2 *Do you agree with Mr Deguchi that it is difficult for teenagers to be very interested in religion? Why do you think this might be?*

3 *What do you think are the advantages and disadvantages of priests or ministers being married as in Japanese and Nying ma pa Buddhism?*

4 *How far do you think learning about different religions and ways of life in school can help to avoid conflict and war?*

5 *Do you think Buddhism is wise to let people continue worshipping their old gods when they become Buddhists?*

6 *Why do you think there are so many festivals for the dead in Japanese Buddhism, when Mr Deguchi says that Buddhism is about this life?*

7 *Drinking tea, making gardens and archery are not usually thought of as religious activities. What connects these Japanese arts with Buddhism?*

section three

FURTHER STUDY

—

Suggestions for further work on Buddhism

—

You might find some of the ideas below helpful in taking your study of Buddhism further. Numbers and letters in brackets refer to useful books and resources in the Bibliography (see pp. 124–130).

1 Compare the ideas and impressions you had of Buddhism and Buddhists before reading this book with those you have now that you have finished reading it. Have there been any changes?

2 Discover from an atlas where the countries listed on p. 4 are to be found. Make a map showing which countries have traditionally followed Buddhism. What do you know about any of these countries?

3 Collect news items concerning Buddhist countries, especially if there is some reference to religion. Burma, Sri Lanka and Tibet often featured in the news when this book was being written.

4 Invite someone who has lived or travelled in a traditionally Buddhist country to speak to your group about life in that country.

5 Choose one Buddhist country and find out more about the geography, history, economics, daily life and religious customs of that country. (4, 9, 10, 13, 19, 26, 34, 36, 48, 49, 51, C, D, E, F, H)

6 Plan a visit to a Buddhist country. Find out how you would travel there, how much it would cost, what time of the year would be best to visit and the main sites and festivals of historical and religious interest you would be able to visit. (d)

7 Find out more about the Buddha's life. There are many books and visual aids to help you. (17, 18, 37, 44, 52, 53, 56, A)

8 Make your own version of the Buddha's life. This could be in the form of a story for young children, a comic book, or a series of pictures for a slide or filmstrip presentation. You need to choose the most significant events of the Buddha's life. (17, 18, 37, 44, 52, 56, A)

9 Discuss the nature of the story of the Buddha's life. Is it history, legend or myth? How far is it possible for us to know the facts about someone who lived so long ago? Do any elements of the story appear to be symbolic rather than literal truth? What does the symbolism tell us about the Buddha? Does it matter whether we know the exact historical facts about the Buddha's life? (17, 18b)

10 Make a collection of different images of the Buddha, in statue or picture form. Note the similarities and differences. Choose your favourite and explain your choice. Discover the meaning of the symbolism in the statues, e.g. the position of the hands. Spend some time sitting quietly and looking at your favourite image, and then express your feelings in poetry or prose. (16, 43, 44, a, b, d, g, iii, iv, v)

11 Buddha images from different countries tend to reflect the features and traditions of people in those countries. Design a Buddha image suitable for modern British Buddhists, and draw, paint or model your image using whatever materials you feel are suitable. (43)

12 Discuss and list the qualities that make a good teacher. Analyse the Buddha's life and teaching and decide what the qualities and techniques were that made him a good teacher.

13 Read some of the stories about the Buddha or that the Buddha told. These could include the stories of the Buddha's previous lives and his famous parables. Try retelling these in a form suitable for young children, as a series of pictures, or even as a drama. (11, 12, 14, 42, 54)

14 Make a collection of Buddhist artefacts (see pp. 129–130; Useful addresses, pp. 131–132).

15 Make a collection of pictures and news items to illustrate the first Noble Truth, that life involves suffering. Use these to make a poster, and think of a suitable title.

16 Make a collection of pairs of pictures illustrating change and impermanence, e.g. a rosebud and a dead rose. Use these to

make a poster, and think of a suitable title.

17 Get everyone in your group to bring in pictures of themselves as babies and as young children. Play 'guess the baby', then use the pictures to make a poster to illustrate the Buddhist teaching that people change as well as things.

18 Discuss what happiness means to you. Draw a 'happiness is . . .' picture. Does anything bring lasting happiness?

19 Make a collection of advertisements that suggest that their product brings happiness. What might a Buddhist have to say about the advertisements' claims? What might a Buddhist think about the effects of advertising on people, both in this country and in poorer countries? How does advertising affect you? Do you think that there should be any control over advertising?

20 Find out about the Tibetan 'Wheel of Life', which presents the Buddha's teaching in picture form. Make your own poster of the Wheel of Life, perhaps sharing the different sections of the poster among your group. (36, 43, iv)

21 Imagine that you are a Buddhist parent living in a country where Buddhism is traditional. Your son or daughter has recently moved to Britain. Write a letter giving him or her advice about how to live a Buddhist life in Britain.

22 Read the Buddha's advice to the young man Sigala. How far does this advice still make sense today? If the Buddha was giving this advice today, what new ways of wasting time and money might be included? Make up a story that illustrates the truth of one of these pieces of advice. (14)

23 Make a list of jobs or careers that a Buddhist would consider to be 'right livelihood'. What jobs would you not expect a Buddhist to do?

24 Find out about King Ashoka. List his main decrees. If Ashoka were alive today, what ten decrees do you think he would make? If you could make ten decrees to govern the behaviour of people in this country, what would they be? (42)

25 Invite a Buddhist to speak to your group about his or her views on a given moral issue, e.g. nuclear weapons, animal rights or abortion. Alternatively, research Buddhist views on these issues (see 23 on abortion and embryo research; Useful addresses, pp. 131–132).

26 If you were setting up a new community on a small British island, what rules and customs would you have?

27 Draw up a list of rules for a school run on Buddhist principles.

28 Write an imaginery account of a day in the life of a Buddhist monk or nun of any specified tradition.

29 Discover some more of the 227 rules for Theravada monks. (11, 34)

30 Find out how the Buddha first came to ordain women and what he said about it. What rules were kept by the original bhikkhunis? How far do you think they were made subordinate to the male bhikkhus? (14, 18, 37)

31 Make a list of what you would gain and what you would give up if you became a Buddhist nun or monk. What would you value most about the monastic lifestyle? What would you miss most about the lay life?

32 Collect pictures of Buddhist temples from around the world. List the similarities and differences that you see.

33 Design an ideal modern monastery for a Buddhist order in Britain. What would you need to include? (35)

34 Arrange a visit to a monastery or Buddhist centre. (Write to the Buddhist Society for an up-to-date list of addresses.)

35 Find out more about the stupa and its symbolism, and the varieties of stupa in the Buddhist world. Draw or make your own stupa. (16, 35, 43, 55)

36 Set up a Buddhist shrine. (35)

37 Find out more about traditional Buddhist symbols and their significance. Draw, paint or make some of these symbols for a display or to decorate your Buddhist shrine. Invent and create your own new symbols for basic Buddhist beliefs. (16, 43, 57)

38 Choose one Buddhist festival and find out more about the customs associated with it. (21, 35, 50, 57, i)

39 Design and make a card for Wesak. (57)

40 Find out about the places of pilgrimage associated with the Buddha in India, Sri Lanka and other mainly Buddhist countries. (30, 35, 45, d)

41 Try some simple forms of meditation, such as breathing meditation, sitting meditation, or metta meditation. (These are described in interviews (2) and (8). More detailed instructions can
be found in 57 and in publications available from Buddhist
groups, such as the booklet *Serene Reflection Meditation* available from Throssel Hole Priory. Buddhists stress that for further
meditation practice, even of these relatively simple forms, you
need the guidance of a reliable meditation teacher.)

42 Learn to identify some of the main bodhisattvas and the symbolism of the images. Collect pictures, statues or badges. Paint your
own thangkas of bodhisattvas. (16, 29, 36, 42, 43, iv, v)

43 Research the life of a famous Buddhist of the past or present, e.g.
Milarepa, Dogen or the Dalai Lama.

44 Plan a video, filmstrip or radio programme about a Buddhist
topic, e.g. the life of the Buddha, the life of a monk, a Buddhist
festival or the main Buddhist teachings. What would you include? Write your script or storyboard. If possible carry this
through to the recording, photographing or filming.

45 You might be feeling that the interviews in this book missed out
many important questions that you would have liked to ask.
Write your own list of questions for a Buddhist. Perhaps you
could go on to arrange an interview and record it on sound or
video tape. This could then be edited as if for a radio or TV
broadcast.

Bibliography and list of audio-visual aids

—

Bibliography

This represents a selection from the material available. More comprehensive bibliographies can be found in 1 below and in Brown, A. (ed.), *World Religions in Education*, available from the Commission for Racial Equality, Elliot House, 10–12 Allington Street, London SW1 5EH.

Section I   For teachers and older students (A level and above)

General

1. Robinson, R. and Johnson, W., *The Buddhist Tradition* (Wadsworth 1970). Best overall survey of Buddhist to date. Rather expensive as American import.

2 Sangharakshita, *A Survey of Buddhism* (Tharpa 1987). Comprehensive survey by the founder of the WBO.

Theravada

3 *Rahula, W., What the Buddha Taught* (Gordon Frazer 1982). Straightforward account of basic Buddhist doctrine by a Theravada monk, with a selection of scripture.

4 Gombrich, *Theravada Buddhism* (Routledge & Kegan Paul 1986). Social history of Theravada Buddhism.

Mahayana

5 Suzuki, D.T., *Outlines of Mahayana Buddhism* (1983, first published 1907). Now rather old, but a useful survey of main beliefs that characterise Mahayana in general. Latest edition published by Schoken Books, N.Y. 1963.

6 Williams, P., *Mahayan Buddhism* (Routledge forthcoming). Expected companion volume to 4 above.

Zen

7 Watts, A. *The Way of Zen* (Penguin 1962). By a famous Western follower of Zen.

8 Kennett, Roshi Jiyu, *Zen is Eternal Life* (Shasta Abbey 1976). History and practice of Zen by a leading Western female Zen master.

Tibetan

9 Trungpa, C. *Cutting Through Spiritual Materialism* (Shambala 1973). By a lama who escaped from Tibet.

10 Snellgrove, D. and Richardson, H., *A Cultural History of Tibet* (Praeger 1968).

Selections of scriptures

11 Conze, E., *Buddhist Scriptures* (Penguin 1969).

12 de Bary, W., *The Buddhist Tradition* (Vintage 1972).

13 Beyer, S., *The Buddhist Experience* (Wadsworth 1974).

14 Woodward, F.L., *Some Sayings of the Buddha* (Oxford University Press 1973).

15 Sangharakshita, *The Eternal Legacy* (Tharpa 1985).

Buddhist art

16 Zwalf, W. (ed.), *Buddhism, Art and Faith* (British Museum 1985).

The life of the Buddha

17 Carrithers, M., *The Buddha* (Oxford University Press 1983).

18 Nanamoli, *The Life of the Buddha According to the Pali Canon* (BPS, Kandy 1978).

Thomas, E., *The Life of the Buddha as Legend and History* (Routledge & Kegan Paul 1975).

Section II For research purposes

General

19 Bechert, H. and Gombrich, R. (eds), *The World of Buddhism* (Thames & Hudson 1984). Expensive but beautifully illustrated reference book on Buddhism, a survey of Buddhist civilisation.

Ethics

20 Saddhatissa, H., *Buddhist Ethics* (Allen & Unwin 1970).

Festivals

21 Brown, A. (ed.), *Festivals in World Religions* (Longman 1986).

Ordination

22 Silcock, T., *A Village Ordination* (Curzon 1980).

Abortion and embryo research

23 Stott, D., *A Circle of Protection for the Unborn* (1986, available from the Sakya Centre, 27 Lilymead Avenue, Knowle, Bristol BS4 2BY).

Milarepa

24 Chang, G.C., *The Hundred Thousand Songs of Milarepa* Harper 1970).

25 Evans-Wentz, W.Y., *Tibet's Great Yogi, Milarepa* (Oxford University Press 1974).

Invasion of Tibet

26 Trungpa, C., *Born in Tibet* (Allen & Unwin 1979). Autobiography of a lama who fled to the West.

Sangharakshita and the WBO

27 Subhuti, *Buddhism for Today* (Element 1983).

28 Sangharakshita, *The Story of My Going for Refuge* (FWBO 1988).

Kwanyin

29 Blofeld, J., *Compassion Yoga* (Mandala 1978).

Pilgrimage

30 Russell, J., *The Eight Places of Buddhist Pilgrimage* (Wisdom 1981).

The history of Buddhism

31 Conze, E., *A Short History of Buddhism* (Unwin 1960).

Buddhism in Britain

32 Humphreys, C., *60 Years of Buddhism in England* (Buddhist Society 1968).

33 Oliver, I., *Buddhism in Britain* (Rider 1979).

Section III   Mainly for GCSE

34 Thompson, M., *Buddhist Teaching and Practice* (Edward Arnold 1985). Good basic summary of the teachings and practices of Buddhism.

35 Morgan, P., *Buddhism in the Twentieth Century* (Hulton 1985). Thematic study of Buddhism especially for GCSE covering the life and teachings of the Buddha, scriptures, worship, pilgrimage and festivals.

36 Morgan, P., *Buddhism* (Batsford 1987). In the Dictionaries of World Religions series, containing all main topics for GCSE syllabuses in easy reference form.

37 Saddhatissa, *The Life of the Buddha* (Unwin 1976).

38 Ling, T., *Buddhism* (Ward Lock 1973). Inexpensive brief booklet on Theravada Buddhism.

39 Pye, M., *Zen and Modern Japanese Religion* (Ward Lock 1973).

Inexpensive brief booklet on Japanese Buddhism.

40 Naylor, D., *Thinking about Buddhism* (Lutterworth 1976). Useful introduction to Buddhism.

41 Reps, P., *Zen Flesh, Zen Bones* (Pelican 1977). Collection of Zen stories, often amusing.

Section IV   For younger children but with useful stories, pictures and information for older students and busy teachers

42 Morgan, P., *Buddhist Stories* (available from P. Morgan at Westminster College, Oxford). Very useful collection of Buddhist stories, including Jataka stories and an explanation of the bodhisattva Chenrezi.

43 Morgan, P., *Buddhist Iconography* (available from P. Morgan at Westminster College, Oxford). Useful collection of line drawings and explanations of Buddha statues, stupas, the Wheel of Life, Chenrezi, Bodhidharama, Kwanyin and other symbols.

44 Naylor, D., *The Buddha, a Journey* (Macmillan 1987). Life and teaching of the Buddha presented in a way that allows pupils to be actively involved (plenty of 'think spots' and 'things to do').

45 Bancroft, A., *The Buddhist World* (Macdonald 1984). For junior/lower secondary, packed with excellent colour pictures.

46 Ascott, J., *Our Buddhist Friends* (Denholm 1978). Aimed at primary children, looks at the beliefs and practices of a Sri Lankan family in Britain.

47 Samarasekara, *I am a Buddhist* (Franklin Watts 1986). Udeni is a ten-year-old girl from a Sri Lankan family resident in Britain. Family customs illustrated in colour.

48 Bennet, G., *Sri Lanka* (A & C Black 1980). In the Beans series. An 11-year-old Sri Lankan boy in a village in Sri Lanka.

49 Barker, C., *Ananda in Sri Lanka* (Hamish Hamilton 1979). Life of a boy in Sri Lanka. It is often commented that this book seems a little idealised in view of the communal conflicts in Sri Lanka since 1983.

50 Bancroft, A., *Festivals of the Buddha* (RMEP 1984), In the Living Festivals series.

51 Davidson, A., *Wedding in Laos* (Cambridge University Press 1982).

52 Landaw, J., *Prince Siddhartha* (Wisdom 1980). Beautifully illustrated children's version of the Buddha's life.

53 Association of Buddhist Women, *The Story of the Buddha* (available from the London Buddhist Vihara, 5 Heathfield Gardens, Chiswick, London W4 4JU). Well-illustrated and very inexpensive.

54 Snelling, J., *Ten Buddhist Fables* (available from the Buddhist Publishing Group, P.O. Box 136, Leicester LE2).

55 Penney, S., *Buddhism* (Heinemann 1989). In the Discovering Religion series, designed for less able secondary students but with useful illustrations and activities for students of all ages and abilities.

56 Hunt, D., *The Buddha* (Oliver & Boyd). In the Leaders of Religions series.

57 Avon County Multicultural Education Centre, *Buddhist Festivals*. (Available from the MEC, Bishop Road, Bishopston, Bristol). Useful pack of information and activities.

58 Snelling, J., *Buddhist Stories* (Wayland 1986).

Audiovisual aids

Videos

A *Buddhism in Focus Part I: Buddha's Life and Teaching* (Meridian/RMEP). Illustrated with slides from 52. Includes a brief visit to the FWBO vegetarian restaurant in London.

B *Buddhism in Focus Part II: The Buddhist Way of Life* (Meridian/RMEP). Rather more interesting than A, visits Theravada, Tibetan and FWBO centres and investigates ceremonies such as dana, meditation and puja. Talks to a young Western boy in a monastery in Nepal, and shows traditional Tibetan monastic debating.

From the BBC

C *The Footprint of the Buddha* (Long Search series 1977). Buddhism in Sri Lanka.

D *The Land of the Disappearing Buddha* (Long Search series 1977). Buddhism in Japan.

E *Buddhism in Thailand* (Everyman series 1985).

F *Buddhism in Laos* (Everyman series 1985).

G *When Buddha came to Sussex* (1979, on loan from Chithurst Buddhist monastery).

H *Norbu's Monastery*. In the Himalayas.

From ITV

I *Buddhist Monk* (Believe It or Not series).

Slides and filmstrips

a *Encounter with Buddhism* (BBC Radiovision).

b *Buddhism* (Concordia Filmstrip).

c *A Visit to the Sakya Centre.* Set of slides, photographs and activities in a pack available from RLDU, Bishop Road, Bishopton, Bristol, BS7 8LS.

d Several sets on places of interest in Sri Lanka and India from Bury Peerless, 22 King's Avenue, Minnis Bay, Burchington, Kent CT7 9QL.

e *Buddhism* (Argus Multimedia Kit).

f *The World's Great Religions: Buddhism* (Time-Life Educational).

g *Buddhism in Britain Today.* A slide series showing the people and places explored in this book is to be available from the author in the near future. Contact D. Cush at Bath College of Higher Education, Newton Park, Newton St Loe, Bath BA2 9BN. A further series on *Buddhism Around the World* is also planned.

Audiotapes

Tapes of chanting and pujas from the various traditions are available from the main Buddhist centres.

Posters

i 'Buddhist Festivals'. Set of four posters with useful notes available from Pictorial Charts Educational Trust.

ii 'Sacred Books: Buddhist'. Two different posters with examples of Pali available from Pictorial Charts Educational Trust.

iii Posters on Buddhist art, e.g. a Zen garden, available from Pictorial Charts Educational Trust.

iv 'The Wheel of Life' and a large variety of mainly Tibetan posters available from Tantra Designs.

v Bodhisattva posters available from Articles of Faith.

Artefacts and postcards

The Buddhism Resource Project is planning to produce a 'Buddhist Artefacts Box' with comprehensive notes in the near future. This package should be less expensive and more 'user-friendly' than collecting individual items. There follows a list of artefacts presently available.

From Tantra Designs: *malas* (prayer beads), 'Wheel of Life' poster, posters of buddhas and bodhisattvas, statues of buddhas and bodhisattvas, an assortment of Buddhist cards, badges, T-shirts, window prints and incense, all from the Tibetan tradition.

From Articles of Faith: malas, Tibetan *dorje* and bell, Tibetan prayer wheel, Buddha statues, posters.

From Wisdom: Wisdom prints, cards.

From Throssel Hole Priory: complete altar sets, malas, calligraphy cards, zafus (meditation cushions), statues.

From Bristol Buddhist Centre: handcarved wooden stupas, badges, puja book.

Most Buddhist centres will have some cards and artefacts.

Useful addresses

—

1 Amaravati Buddhist Centre, Great Gaddesden, Hemel Hempstead, Hertfordshire, HP1 3BZ. A main Theravada centre.

2 Angulimala: Buddhist Prison Chaplaincy Organisation: Ven. Khemadhammo, The Forest Hermitage, Lower Fulbrook, Warwick CV35 8AS.

3 Articles of Faith, Sacred Trinity Centre, Chapel Street, Salford M3 7AJ. Supply artefacts, cards, posters.

4 Buddhism Resource Project. A group of teachers, lecturers and Buddhists who are working on the provision of resources for the teaching of Buddhism. The author is a member of the project and this book has been produced with its help. Information is available from Anita Cotterall, Publications and Projects Officer, 44 Doctor's Hill, Stourbridge, West Midlands DY9 0YE.

5 Buddhist Animal Rights Group, 141 Allison Street, Crosshill, Glasgow G42 8RY.

6 Buddhist Hospice Project: Dennis Sibley, 17 Cavendish Place, Newport, Isle of Wight PO30 5AE.

7 Buddhist Peace Fellowship, Dorset Peace Council, The Old George, The Square, Broadwindsor, Beaminster, Dorset DT8 3DQ.

8 Buddhist Society, 58 Eccleston Square, London SW1V 1PH. Founded in 1924 by Christmas Humphreys, the society is committed to no one tradition, but is a useful source of information for all. Among its useful publications are resource lists for teachers and the invaluable *Buddhist Directory*, which gives the addresses of all Buddhist organisations known to the society – there is bound to be one near you!

9 FWBO, Main Order Office, Lesingham House, Surlingham, Norwich NR14 7AL. Bristol Buddhist Centre, 9 Cromwell Road, St Andrews, Bristol BS6 5HD can also supply a puja book, badges and handcarved wooden stupas.

10 Madhyamaka Centre, Kilnwick Percy Hall, Pocklington, York YO4 2UF.

11 Manjusri Institute, Conishead Priory, Ulverston, Cumbria LA12 9QQ. Tibetan Ge lug pa centre. Can supply incense, malas, cards, tapes, texts, etc.

12 Nichiren Shoshu UK, 1 The Green, Richmond, Surrey TW9 1PL.

13 Pictorial Charts Educational Trust, 27 Kitchen Road, London W13 0UD. Supply a huge range of posters for religious education, including a set on Buddhist festivals and individual items in sets on art, sacred books, etc.

14 Tantra Designs, Gas Ferry Road, Bristol BS1 6UN. Supply a huge range of posters, statues, badges, T-shirts, cards, beads, window prints, incense. Send for catalogue.

15 Tharpa Publications, 15 Bendemeer Road, London SW15. Supply books, cards, high-quality prints.

16 Throssel Hole Priory, Carrshield, Hexham, Northumberland NE47 8AL. The main training monastery for Soto Zen. Can supply books, statues and altar requirements, calligraphy cards, zafu cushions, prayer beads, etc. Send for its catalogue.

17 Wisdom Publications, 402 Hoe Street, Walthamstow, London. Supply books on Tibetan Buddhism, cards, posters and prints, calendars, colouring books.

Glossary

—

A ll words in this Glossary are followed by a letter or letters which indicate their language of origin. C = Chinese, E = English, G = Greek, J = Japanese, P = Pali, S = *Sanskrit*, T = Tibetan, Th = Thai.

Ajahn (Th): Title for teacher in Thai Theravada.

Amida (J): A non-historical buddha.

Anagarika (P): A stage half way between lay and monastic (in English, Theravada).

Anatta (P): 'No self', without individual essence.

Anicca (P): Impermanence.

Arhat (P): Enlightened person.

Asala (P): Theravada festival celebrating the first sermon of the Buddha.

Asceticism (E): Living without luxuries, penance.

Avalokitesvara (S): Bodhisattva of compassion.

Ayya (Th): 'Sister', Thai word for nun.

BCE (E): Before the Common Era, equivalent to BC but without the Christian doctrinal statement.

Bhikkhu (P): Monk.

Bhikkhuni (P): Nun.

Bodhidharma (S): Legendary founder of Zen.

Bodhisattva (S): 'Being of enlightenment'. 1 A being who dedicates him/herself to obtaining enlightenment not for him/herself but in order to help others. 2 Gautama Buddha in his life/lives previous to enlightenment.

Buddha (P, S): 'Enlightened one', 'enlightened being'.

Butsu dan (J): Buddhist shrine.

Calligraphy (E): Ornate writing, an art form.

CE (E): Common Era, equivalent to AD but without the Christian doctrinal statement.

Chenrezi (T): Bodhisattva of compassion.

Dalai Lama (T): 'Ocean lama', religious leader of Tibetan Buddhists.

Dana (P, S): 'Giving', usually of food to monks.

Dengyo Daishi (J): Founder of Tendai in Japan.

Dhamma (P): Truth, Teaching, Law, Buddhism.

Dharma (S): Truth, Teaching, Law, Buddhism.

Dogen (J): Founder of Japanese Soto Zen.

Dorje (T): Vajra or thunderbolt, ritual implement.

Dukkha (P, S): Suffering, unsatisfactoriness.

Eightfold Path (E): List summarising the Buddhist path: right view, intention, speech, conduct, livelihood, effort, mindfulness and contemplation.

Eight Precepts (E): The Five Precepts plus fasting after midday, wearing no adornments and going to no amusements, and having no luxurious bed.

Five Precepts (E): Not to kill, steal, lie, misuse sex or take intoxicants.

FWBO (E): Friends of the Western Buddhist Order, a new Buddhist movement.

Gelong (T): Monk.

Gelug pa (T): A tradition of Tibetan Buddhism.

Genyen (T): Trainee monk.

Getsu (T): Novice monk.

Gohonzon (J): Scroll containing mandala of Nichiren's mantra.

Gojukai (J): Initiation, especially in Nichiren Buddhism.

Gompa (T): Shrine or meditation room.

Gongyo (J): Recitation.

Guru (S): Teacher who passes on religious tradition.

Guru Rinpoche (S, T): 'Precious guru', a title for Padmasambhava.

Higan (J): Japanese equinox festival (March and September). The dead are remembered.

Hinayana (S): 'Small vehicle', Mahayana term for non-Mahayana Buddhist traditions.

Ihai (J): Memorial tablet for the dead.

Jataka (P): Stories of previous lives of the Buddha.

Jewels, Three (E): The Buddha, the Dharma and the Sangha.

Jukai (J): Lay ordination in Soto Zen.

Juzu (J): Prayer beads, malas.

Kanzeon (J): Japanese form of Avalokitesvara.

Kargyu pa (T): Tradition of Tibetan Buddhism.

Karma (S): 'Actions', the law of cause and effect. Good actions bring happiness, bad actions brings unhappiness.

Kata (T): White silk scarf, sign of respect.

Kathina (P): Ceremony of presenting special robe.

Kesa (J): Small stole representing monk's robe, also wakesa.

Ketchimyaku (J): Scroll showing lineage of teachers.

Kinhin (J): Walking meditation.

Koan (J): 'Case', saying of a Zen master.

Kwannon (J): Japanese form of Kwanyin.

Kwanyin (C): Female bodhisattva of compassion.

Lama (T): Tibetan name for guru.

Lay (E): A follower of a religion who is not a monk, nun, priest or other religious specialist.

Lotus Sutra (E, S): An important Mahayana sutra.

Lung (T): Ritual transmission of a sacred text.

Magha Puja (P): Thai festival celebrating the Sangha.

Mahayana (S): 'Great vehicle', one of the two main wings of Buddhist tradition.

Mala (S): Prayer beads.

Mandala (S): Circular coloured diagram.

Manjusri (S): Bodhisattva of wisdom.

Mantra (S): A sacred syllable or short series of these.

Marks of Life, Three (E): Anicca, dukkha and anatta.

Meditation (E): Concentration, any technique which trains the mind, usually in a religious context.

Merit (E): Good karma.

Metta (P): Loving kindness, friendly love.

Mindfulness (E): Awareness, a meditation practice.

Mitra (S): A friend (a term used in FWBO).

Mudra (S): A symbolic shape made with the hands.

Nibbana (P): 'Blown out', the state where all greed, hatred and delusion are ended, eternal peace.

Nichiren (J): Thirteenth-century monk who started Nichiren Shoshu.

Nichiren Shoshu (J): A Japanese Buddhist tradition.

Nirvana (S): Sanskrit for nibbana.

Nying ma pa (T): Tradition of Tibetan Buddhism.

Obon (J): Japanese festival welcoming spirits of ancestors home.

Padmasambhava (S): A famous enlightened person who established Buddhism in Tibet.

Pali (P): Acient Indian language used in Theravada scriptures.

Pali Canon (P, E): The scriptures of Theravada Buddhism.

Patimokkha The list of 227 rules for Theravada monks recited every fortnight.

Pirit (P): Sections of the Pali Canon chanted as a blessing.

Poson (P): Sri Lankan festival.

Prajnaparamita (S): 'Perfect wisdom', also a series of Mahayana scriptures.

Puja (S): Devotional ceremony.

Pure Land (E): Tradition of Buddhism centred on devotion to Amida.

Rebirth (E): Doctrine that we pass through many lives in samsara.

Refuges, Three (E): Pledging of commitment to the Three Jewels.

Rinzai (J): Tradition within Zen.

Sakyamuni (S): *See* Shakyamuni.

Sakya pa (T): Tradition of Tibetan Buddhism.

Samanera a novice, or the early stage in monastic life before becoming a full monk. No-one under 20 years of age can progress past samanara ordination.

Samsara (S, P): The cycle of existence, rebirths into unsatisfactory states, ordinary unenlightened life.

Sangha (S, P): 'Assembly', the Buddhist community, sometimes restricted to the community of monastics only.

Sanskrit (S): Ancient Indian language of Hinduism and many Mahayana scriptures.

Satori (J): Zen word for moment of enlightenment.

Sesshin (J): Zen meditation retreat.

Shakyamuni (S): Wise man of the Shakya tribe, another name for the Buddha.

Siddhartha Gautama (S): Personal name of the historical Buddha.

Siddhatta Gotama (P): Personal name of the historical Buddha.

Sima (P): Ritual boundary of monastery.

Soka Gakkai (J): A Japanese lay movement associated with the Nichiren Shoshu.

Soto (J): A tradition within Zen.

Stupa (P): Monument over Buddhist relics.

Sutra (S): Scripture.

Sutta (P): Scripture.

Tantra (S): Scriptures of Vajrayana Buddhism and parallel movements in Hinduism.

Tantric (E): Buddhism based on tantra texts and related practices.

Tara (S): A female bodhisattva.

Tendai (J): A Japanese tradition of Buddhism related to Chinese Tien tai.

Terma (T): Ornate offering made of butter or marzipan.

Thangka (T): Tibetan religious painting on cloth.

Theosophical Society (E): Religious organisation founded in the USA drawing on ideas from Eastern religions.

Theravada (P, S): 'The way of the elders', one of the two main wings of Buddhist tradition.

Thero (P): Senior monk of over ten years in the robes.

Trikaya (S): Mahayana doctrine that Buddha has three forms:

human, glorious and pure mind (nirmanakaya, sambhogakaya and dharmakaya).

Tulku (T): A bodhisattva in human form, taking several rebirths which can be identified (*see* trikaya).

Unsui (J): 'Free as the clouds', a monk.

Upaya (S): 'Means' (short for upaya kausalya, 'skilful means'), the ability to know exactly what to do for the best in all situations. May involve 'bending the rules' or 'being economical with the truth'.

Vajra (S): 'Diamond' or 'thunderbold', ritual implement used in Vajrayana.

Vajrayana (S): 'Diamond or thunderbolt vehicle', name used to distinguish Tantric Buddhism from other forms of Mahayana. Sometimes seen as a third, separate 'yana' of Buddhism and sometimes applied rather loosely to the whole of Tibetan Buddhism.

Vassa (P): Three months' rainy season retreat.

Vihara (P): Buddhist monastery or temple.

Vinaya (P): The discipline section of the Pali Canon dealing with rules for monks.

Visualisation (E): Meditation technique, focusing on a particular mental image.

Wakesa (J): Small stole symbolising the monk's robe, also kesa.

Wa Shu (J): Japanese 'harmony' sect.

WBO (E): Western Buddhist Order, a new religious movement.

Wesak (P): Theravada festival celebrating the birth, enlightenment and death of the Buddha.

Zafu (J): Meditation cushion.

Zazen (J): Sitting meditation.

Zen (J): A tradition of Buddhism.

Zendo (J): Meditation room or shrine room.

Index